INTERNATIONAL DEVELOPMENT FROM A KINGDOM PERSPECTIVE

EDITED BY
JAMES BUTARE-KIYOVU

WILLIAM CAREY INTERNATIONAL UNIVERSITY PRESS

wciu
press

William Carey International University Press

1539 E. Howard St.
Pasadena, California 91104
Email: wciupress_orders@wciu.edu

James Butare-Kiyovu, Editor
International Development from a Kingdom Perspective

WCIU Press: International Development Series Number Two

Library of Congress Control Number: 2010922127

ISBN: 978-0-86585-028-6

Printed in the United States of America

CONTENTS

GENERAL INTRODUCTION: MISSIONS AND INTERNATIONAL DEVELOPMENT

James Butare-Kiyovu

In Luke 4: 18-19, Jesus gave us a master plan of action for *Doing God's Will on Earth*. Luke recorded that, reading from Prophet Isaiah, Jesus found a place where it is written:

"The Spirit of the Lord is upon me,
For he has appointed me to preach
Good News to the poor.
He has sent me to proclaim
That captives will be released,
That the blind will see,
That the downtrodden will be freed
From their oppressors,
And that the time of the Lord's
Favor has come."

A Fourth Era of Missions

Ralph Winter, the founder of the Frontier Mission Fellowship (FMF) and the two sister organizations, US Center for World Mission (USCWM) and WCIU, wrote an article entitled "Four Men, Three Eras, Two Transitions: Modern Missions" which gives a good historical background to modern missions.

On December 21, 2007, Ralph Winter gave a seminar entitled "Is There a Fourth Era?" At the end of the seminar, he stated that,

to refer to a Fourth Era is not yet an institutional decision. But it is certainly a substantial subject to talk about—the idea of a fourth era of far larger mission challenge than ever before. It applies to this country, and to every other country. It applies to all Perspectives students, not just those who go into full-time "Christian ministry.

In his revised article "Three Mission Eras, And the Loss and Recovery of Kingdom Mission, 1800–2000," he briefly mentions the "Fourth Era" on page 44 of this book.

In suggesting a 4th Era of Missions, Ralph Winter said he was revising his article in earlier versions of the *Perspectives* book which is called "Four Men, Three Eras: Carey, Taylor, Townsend and McGavran," in which he argues that,

> [w]e have potentially a world-wide network of churches that can be aroused to their central mission. Best of all, nothing can obscure the fact that this could and should be the final era. No serious believer today dare overlook the fact that God has asked us to reach every nation, tribe and tongue without intending it to be done. No generation has less excuse than ours if we do not do as He asks.

Why a 4th Era of Missions?

After a brief historical background, Ralph Winter pointed out during the seminar that "[t]oday everywhere you look, people are not merely talking about doing little good deeds but talking about dealing with things like world poverty and world problems to an extent that has not ever been seen." He talked about a desperate need to have a more faithful understanding of the Bible than ever before. "Is it not time, then, to name this Era, 'the Kingdom Era', the fourth era? As in the earlier eras, everything preceding is still included. When we went inland we didn't stop going to the coastlands. When we went to the unreached peoples we didn't stop going to the major unreached peoples."

In an earlier article which appeared in *Mission Frontiers*, November-December 2007, Ralph Winter had this to say:

> Is it good enough simply to make people feel secure in this life and hopeful about eventually getting out of this sin-filled world and safely through the pearly gates? Right now that is the main thing the church is doing. In stark contrast are those tasks like restoring

creation, restoring God's glory, rediscovering Satan's works, and deliberately destroying his deeds and deadly delusions. Are we trying to win a war simply by caring for the wounded? The fruits of evil—the sickness, poverty, illiteracy and inhumanity—draw our attention away from the roots of evil.

This is a "wartime" and Biblical perspective, yet that fact has apparently evaporated into the thin air of the current mood, which is defined by an artificial and inadequate (albeit pervasive) peacetime mentality and mandate. *The Biblical mandate is "the Gospel of the Kingdom,"—meaning the extension of that "Rule" against all evil opposition. It is not merely a "Gospel of Salvation." The Gospel of the Kingdom is the central mandate of God's "will being done on earth as it is in heaven." It is a mandate that is distinctly larger than getting along in this life with the help of business, and getting to heaven with the help of missions. God's glory is at stake and His glory is our main business.* [italics mine] (p. 13)

Fourth Era, 1947—Onwards: The Kingdom Era

In his article, page 44, Ralph Winter suggests that pioneers of this Fourth Era are: Karl F. H. Henry (author of *The Uneasy Conscience of Modern Fundamentalism*), Timothy Smith (author of *Revivalism and Social Reform*) and David O. Moberg (author of *The Great Reversal*). Ralph Winter is among these key leaders recognizing a new Era before us. In my opinion, the main characteristics of the Fourth Era are:

1. The Recovery of Church Mission through Kingdom Mission

2. Fighting Evil (including eradicating major diseases such as AIDS and malaria)

International Development and WCIU

As mentioned earlier, the passage Jesus read in Luke 4:18-19 is the master plan of missions and international development. It is an invitation for his followers to join in the restoration of God's *Shalom*. Our obedience pleases Him and restores His Glory on Earth.

I am a faculty member at the William Carey International University, in Pasadena, California, where I have been based since July 2002. WCIU serves a fairly well-defined constituency of non-governmental organizations (NGOs). All WCIU students are required to study *the historical, social, cultural, religious, educational, economic, technical, and political matrix in which they work.*

WCIU defines International Development as an integrated academic field involving all the different disciplines mentioned above, and this is a view I support. The University's unique approach to International Development is quite evident in the MA and Ph.D. curriculum that systematically prepares men and women to discover and address the roots of human problems wherever they are. Many distinguished scholars and many ordinary men and women have contributed to the curriculum, but it is, without doubt, Dr. Winter's missiological approach and his approach to International Development that lies at the heart of the curriculum.

I have also had the privilege of attending several conferences bringing together different organizations involved in missions and international development. In this book, you will find articles by individuals (or by organizations) I have had the privilege to interact with.

Missio Dei
By Eddie Arthur

Eddie Arthur's article traces the history of the term *missio Dei* up to today. He explains how *missio Dei* is closely tied to the Kingdom of God. The article clarifies the relationships between missio Dei and the Church, missio Dei and other Religions, and Evangelicals and missio Dei before focusing on the central theme of the *Trinitarian Mission.*

Eddie Arthur makes two important points which are key to understanding the concept of International Development in this book:

1. On page 60 he says,

> In becoming a man, Jesus became poor and spent a lot of time with the poor, and focusing on the needs of the poor is an intrinsic part of God's purposes for the Church.

2. On pages 61 he says,

> The Trinitarian focus on *missio Dei,* combined with the focus on the Kingdom of God rescues the Church from simply becoming an agent for social and economic change on the one hand or fundamentalism on the other and provides a framework for mission in which the false dichotomy between social action and evangelism in mission can be eradicated.

Holistic Help for the Peoples of This Earth: from Sudan to Switzerland
By Kirk Franklin

Kirk Franklin makes two statements that are relevant to the main theme of this book.

> Statement #1: The mission of Jesus was carried out through his words, deeds and signs, and the people he focused on were often the poor and marginalized.

> Statement #2: As followers of Jesus, Wycliffe personnel focus on minority people groups so that they can hear God talk in their language.

Kirk Franklin starts by "identifying the problem" and then focuses on "addressing the issues through various partnerships." This is similar to WCIUs institutional mission of preparing men and women to discover and address the roots of human problems around the world. Note that the title of Franklin's article is "Holistic Help for *the Peoples of This Earth: from Sudan to Switzerland.*"

Kirk Franklin practices what he preaches, namely: finding solutions outside the box. He quotes Albert Einstein's statement, "No problem can be solved from the same level of consciousness that created it," and concludes that solutions for problems of this magnitude do not get found just by looking within the systems that created them. The solutions may lie elsewhere. Ralph Winter also shared and practiced this trait of finding solutions outside the box.

Kirk Franklin discusses the concept of *Shalom* where "the answer lies." This is similar to the solution proposed in Beth Snodderly's article, "The Goal of the Kingdom and of International Development." Kirk Franklin also makes reference to the Micah Network and the concept of "integral mission" which is also found in the Micah Challenge Prayer Guide on the Millennium Development Goals (MDGs) article.

The case study on the Lamnso of Northwest Cameroon, "Can a community of *shalom* be an outgrowth of a Bible translation project?" is a good example of how Bible Translation and Literacy bring about transformational change and international development—a connection that may not be so obvious to some.

Shalom: The Goal of the Kingdom and of International Development
By Beth Snodderly

Beth Snodderly quotes from a report aired on the television current affairs show "60 Minutes" on a rape situation in the war-torn Democratic Republic of Congo (DRC), and compares the conditions of this society to a society described in Isaiah 59: 4-11. She then asks four questions that are explained in the rest of the article.

1. What is wrong with these two societies? How do societies get to the place where such unrestrained violence and corruption break out?

2. What does God want human life to look like?

3. What are the essential conditions for a society to experience wholeness, peace and safety?

4. What is the responsibility of the body of Christ to those in harm's way? What should be the role of Kingdom-minded international development workers in addressing the roots of human problems around the world and what opposition should they expect to face?

I agree with Beth Snodderly's application of the Biblical concept of *Shalom*. I also agree that the main problems are the *"interest groups"* that will stop at nothing in order to rape the natural resources of the land. The raping of women is one of many tactics used to intimidate the helpless victims who live in places such as Congo and Sudan. As many people have observed, natural resources have become a curse instead of a blessing for the inhabitants of countries rich in oil, coltan and other minerals. An internet search of the phrase "Congo's Bloody Coltan" comes up with a video report produced by Pulitzer Center that provides a compelling argument of the root causes of the war in DRC.

Economic Justice for the Poor
By David Befus and Stephan Bauman

The article establishes a solid Biblical foundation of economic justice and then goes on to demonstrate the Church's mandate "to embrace, pursue, and model economic justice." The article ends with a comprehensive list of "action plans" of how the writers exhort the Church to act.

Development Is Like a River
By Karl J. Franklin

Karl Franklin uses parables, personal experience and humor to describe some of the problems associated with development. He compares development to a river and uses a humorous illustration of a water-bottling parable to show a number of things that go wrong when people are trying to come up with "solutions" without proper diagnosis of the root problems. A good reminder to all of us involved in projects is that a lot of money floating down a "river" will not necessarily address the problems of development.

Discovering and Addressing the Root Causes of Genocide in Rwanda
By James Butare

My goals in this paper are, first of all, to suggest some historical, cultural and socio-political issues that are at the root of the Rwandan Genocide and then to identify a way of addressing the root problem.

Millennium Development Goals Prayer Guide: Micah Declaration on Integral Mission
By Micah Challenge

A key excerpt which Kirk Franklin's article also refers to, reads:
> Integral mission or holistic transformation is the proclamation and demonstration of the gospel. It is not simply that evangelism and social involvement are to be done alongside each other. Rather, in integral mission our proclamation has social consequences as we call people to love and repentance in all areas of life. And our social involvement has evangelistic consequences as we bear witness to the transforming grace of Jesus Christ. If we ignore the world, we betray the word of God which sends us out to serve the world. If we ignore the word of God, we have nothing to bring to the world. Justice and justification by faith, worship and political action, the spiritual and the material, personal change and structural change belong together. As in the life of Jesus, being, doing and saying are at the heart of our integral task.

Micah Challenge is grounded in the spirit of Micah 6:8, "And what does the Lord require of you? To act justly and to love mercy and to walk humbly with your God."

Participants in the Micah Challenge welcome the UN initiative on the Millennium Development Goals and pledge to back this with prayer and practical actions as suggested in the prayer guide/article.

THREE MISSION ERAS, AND THE LOSS AND RECOVERY OF KINGDOM MISSION, 1800–2000

Ralph D. Winter

I t is a huge intellectual task to give a brief but fair summary of the last two centuries. In this period more people by far lived, did more things and did more significant things for the Kingdom of God than in all previous history. These years display the roots of a contemporary world more subject to Biblical influence than ever in the human story. What actually happened?

Introduction

Most treatments of this period either leave out the Christian dynamics or the secular events. Putting these two together is the overriding purpose of this essay.

Jesus said, "I will build My Church and the gates of hell will not be able to resist it (Matt 16:18)." Down through history many great traditions, Orthodox, Catholic, Lutheran, Anglican and Presbyterian have, to some great extent in their actions (even if at variance with their theology), understood this verse to be primarily a call for the extension of the Church as an institution rather than the extension of the Kingdom of God and His will on earth (and much less the idea of a militant Church as God's instrument in a war). There is a big difference. For one thing, while the Church must try not to incorporate unbelievers (although it often has), the Kingdom may at times involve reborn church people working together with people outside the Church who do not yet believe, but who may agree on evils to be fought.

We Evangelicals tend to overlook the New Testament phrase *Gospel of God*, which occurs even more frequently than *Gospel of the Kingdom*. By contrast, we seem to be more interested in a *Gospel of Man* whereby getting more members into the Church or more people saved becomes more important than all other ways of *glorifying God.* Today we have new opportunities and resources by which God's Kingdom can be advanced and His Name glorified. Those opportunities do not replace evangelism but make it more credible.

In the last 200 years we see not only a great acceleration of global population, but also a still greater impact of the Biblical revelation, the expansion of the Church and the extension of God's Rule—His Kingdom. Those who yield to the latter as members of His Church emerge in wildly new colors and dimensions, with new insights both good and not so good, and sometimes with conflicts of perspective. We want to see Christianity as it really is. Otherwise we may be inconveniently surprised by the future.

We will see that new movements may be partial, off balance, perhaps heretical. Mission vision and strategy have also changed. The Bible, although interpreted differently, is nevertheless the one stable element.

Leading up to these last two explosive centuries there were certain epoch-making events that continue to be major factors in our understanding of mission today.

Significant Prior Events

For example, after 1450, due to the printing press, the Bible and other Christian literature became a flood of influence, undergirding the breakdown (called *The Reformation*) of the long-standing but incorrect assumption by most Mediterranean

Latin-speaking believers, *that the expansion of the faith would and should continue to be clothed in a Mediterranean culture.* That of course did not happen. Although for many centuries the Latin language had helpfully united scholars over a huge territory, what had long been seen to be culturally "the seamless robe of Christ" became a much more complex checkered garment. At the same time, it has become a pluralistic reality capable of infusing any and every cultural tradition, a treasure capable of being carried in any number of "earthen vessels."

Secondly, what Andrew Walls has called "The Great European Migration" expanded out into the entire globe. That began to happen at the moment Columbus, in 1492, "sailed the ocean blue."

Thirdly, a phenomenon more important for our topic is the fact that, along with commercial expansion, the Latin branch of the faith (with both its strengths and weaknesses, newly reenergized before, during and after the Reformation) also expanded significantly between 1600 and 1800, plying the ocean waterways with its devout and determined troops—Franciscan, Dominican, and Jesuit.

Basic Concepts

Coming into view in the last two hundred years are *Three Protestant Mission Eras,* each reflecting new strategies in the global expansion of the Kingdom of God, or at least the Church of God. In order to describe these eras, and for the purposes of this chapter, I employ two phrases: 1) *Church Mission*, which I define as the winning of people into the Church wherever in the world, and thus *extending the membership of the Church*, and 2) *Kingdom Mission*, which we define as the work of the church beyond itself, going beyond *Church Mission* to see that His will is done on earth outside the Church. This is *the extension of the Kingdom of God. Church Mission* is basic and essential but must not become merely a goal in itself. It must be seen also as a means of relentlessly pressing for God's will to be done on earth, thus to declare His glory among all peoples.

In light of these two coinages, *Church Mission* and *Kingdom Mission*, The Great Commission clearly includes both (not just "foreign missions," or Kingdom Mission) for that is certainly what is meant by "teaching them to obey everything I have commanded you (Matt. 28:20)." Granted that it is more common to distinguish between home and foreign missions, or between monocultural *evangelism* and the highest priority—pioneer, crosscultural evangelism or *mission*. In this chapter, both Church Mission and Kingdom Mission must be involved both at home and abroad, both where the Church already is and where it is not yet.

The Three Eras in Brief

The First Era, 1800 to 1910, followed the much-delayed conversion of Protestant Christianity to missions. In that conversion Protestantism went from being merely a profoundly religious and semi-political movement to a sudden awareness of global mission, both Church and Kingdom Mission. In a sense the conversion took roughly 300 years, from 1500 to 1800. However, in the last few years before the year 1800 Protestant mission awareness accelerated very rapidly on the surfboard of the Evangelical Awakening.

This accelerated understanding generated the First Era of Protestant missions, which was, in a sense, the William Carey Era. William Carey was, for Protestants, the one who both led the way out of Europe to the *coastlands* of the world, but also, as a true heir of the Evangelical Awakening, promoted a broad Kingdom of God approach. Those many who followed his lead reflected the same very wide spectrum of his concern for both evangelism and cultural transformation, for both Church and Kingdom Mission. (See the fascinating chapter on Carey by the Mangalwadis). Many missionaries in the remainder of the 19th century followed his example of founding a university to promote general knowledge and truth.

The Second Era, 1865–1980, introduced what became a distinct polarization between those concerned about personal salvation and those eager to see "the Kingdom come on earth." The polarization was already evident by 1900, but especially so in the Fundamentalist/Modernist controversies of the 1920s. In American missions and churches, in this period, we often see an unfortunate choice between 1) Kingdom Mission, which involved the Church being salt and light, glorifying God in all the earth, doing so by (what was called in those days) "civilizing" *as well as* Church Mission—evangelizing and expanding the church, and 2) Church Mission alone, which in missions became the activity of mission agencies mainly drawing on Bible institute graduates and other non-college people representing less influential families, primarily emphasizing a heaven-oriented, personal fulfillment gospel intended mainly to draw people into Church membership.

The enforced choice of this polarization was then an artificial tension between saving souls and saving souls *plus* saving people, society, and nature. This divergence extended well into, and became virulent in, the 20th century. Note, "civilizing" in those days did not mean fostering etiquette but helping people become literate and make a living, plus ending cannibalism, foot binding, widow burning, and female infanticide.

For example, Hudson Taylor, representing roughly the evangelism-only pole of the controversy (*Church Mission* alone), began bravely and indefatigably penetrating the *inland* territories of China, not only creating what was eventually the largest mission to China, the China Inland Mission (now Overseas Missionary Fellowship), but encouraging into existence fourteen other inland-emphasizing missions—against considerable opposition. Incidentally, opposition to his going *inland* died down much sooner than the polarization between "civilizing" and evangelism, between Kingdom Mission and mere Church Mission. Other significant missionaries to China worked along very different lines, as we shall see.

The Third Era, 1935 to present, is characterized in two ways, 1) Townsend and McGavran's discovery, respectively, of the need for Bible translation in tribal groups, and the importance of creating a "Christward movement" within a specific "ethne," especially those already penetrated by "a Bridge of God" (one or more believers within an otherwise unpenetrated group). A further development was the additional concern for all the world's smaller, by-passed ethnic groups—those not already penetrated, "Unreached Peoples." Note that the concern of this Era is not just the winning of numbers of individuals, and not just thinking in terms of geopolitical definitions of countries, coastlands or inland territories. The Third Era also began to reflect, 2) a gradual and welcome, crucial healing of the heaven vs. earth polarization inherited from the final years of the Second Era.

These two dimensions are still unfolding. However, Kingdom Mission, and thus the idea of a Kingdom Era, is coming to the fore, potentially uniting the two.

It is important to realize that what is happening in no way should be allowed to obscure the priority for the evangelization of Unreached Peoples. Indeed, rightly understood, evangelism in word, *if supported by "demonstration" in* deed, *is actually empowered evangelism. It seems obvious that the highest priority should be to go where the darkness is deepest. That, in turn, means clearly to go to those places where Jesus is not yet known. That, then, means we are still talking about the priority of reaching out to the thousands of remaining "Unreached Peoples."*

THE FIRST ERA: 1800–1910
Coastlands, Kingdom Mission

Protestant missions began about the time Catholics pulled back for other reasons. By roughly 1800 the French Revolution and its Napoleonic aftermath left Europe in shambles, cutting the roots of the global European commercial and Catholic missionary exploits. What saved both England and America from the European fate was the powerful, earlier, transatlantic Evangelical Awakening (in America called "The Great Awakening in the Middle Colonies"). By the end of the era at the great World Missionary Conference at Edinburgh of 1910 there was no longer any doubt about the legitimacy of Protestant missions.

However, the next, Second Era, had already begun years earlier in 1865. In the 45-year overlapping period (1865-1910) significant tension existed due to the divergent missiologies (understandings of mission) appropriate in older fields of mission work and what was appropriate to new beginnings where there were no churches. In this transition there was also the beginning of the polarization between Church Mission alone and Church Mission plus Kingdom mission, as we shall see.

Revival, Diversity and Hostility

It is important to recognize that religious advance, whether in the Western or the non-Western worlds, may indirectly produce undesirable results. Note, for example, that the ominous and ghastly French Revolution had been largely triggered by the American Revolution. Both revolutions released people from authority. But the revolution in America, by contrast, was largely sparked and fueled by the momentous Great Awakening. This seaboard awakening vastly expanded the number of both Baptists and Presbyterians, extending the latter as a single, democratic structure reaching from Boston to Charleston. In 1789 the U. S. Constitution and a revised Presbyterian constitution were being written two blocks apart by many of the same men and with much of the same wording. Little did the Americans of the Great Awakening realize that their wonderful dreams would become French nightmares in a few short years. Why? French society had not been honeycombed by local democratic congregations as in England and America. The desirable aspects of the transplanted American experience for that reason could not take root in French soil. Even in America the Revolution was almost taken over by nonreligious multitudes.

For example, by 1800, the French revolutionary hysteria also ran powerfully in America. Not everyone released from British authority wanted to be under God's authority. At Yale, in 1800 the largest school of higher education in the USA, the godly president, Timothy Dwight (grandson of the influential Evangelical minister Jonathan Edwards) had to allow the handful of openly Christian students at Yale to pray right inside his office. That was the only place safe from the vast majority of hostile, anti-religious students. Some of those students were calling themselves by the names of leading French Revolutionaries—Danton, Robespierre, Marat, Hébert.

In 1806 the famous "Haystack" students at Williams College faced similar hostility being forced to pray outdoors because on campus they were totally outnumbered by anti-Christian, revolutionary-minded students. (Note: Not even wanting to come in out of the rain, they sat under the shelter of a haystack that looked like a huge mushroom after cows had eaten around it.)

We see further hostility when "Citizen Genet," an emissary of revolutionary France, landed in Charleston in 1793, and mobs of thousands favoring the French type of violent revolution, even the assassination of George Washington, gathered in ever larger numbers as Genet moved north toward the capitol. Even people on the Western frontier were carrying around miniature guillotines symbolizing what they thought ought to happen to George Washington. But that did not quite come to pass.

Meanwhile, in an England which was not so totally disrupted by the Revolutionary War as were the seceding colonies, the Evangelical Awakening continued to be a major force. The British evangelist George Whitefield had already contributed much to the extensive impact of the Great Awakening in America. Both he and John Wesley were even more prominent in the English Awakening. Wesley was a very determined little man and an impelling evangelist. He was an equally serious and unflinching social reformer, very clearly involved in Kingdom Mission as well as Church Mission.

His converts were prohibited from smuggling, even though that was a way of life for many who lived on the Cornwall peninsula (a long coastland attracting ships from France). But he insisted on *changing* instead of *breaking* the law. His reforms affected orphanages, mental institutions, mines, courts, and Parliament. On his deathbed he wrote William Wilberforce urging him to fight slavery. Wesley, Wilberforce and Carey had all been inspired by the Evangelical Awakening. A letter from Carey, after he was in India, urged a member of Parliament to join the Committee to Abolish Slavery. Furthermore, the specific example of William Carey's mission to India, and his published *Enquiry*, was much of the impulse behind hundreds of others who went to the field, including the five "Haystack" students of 1806. Before they left for the field they promoted the founding of the first foreign mission agency in the USA, the American Board of Commissioners for Foreign Missions (ABCFM), in 1812.

Secondary Impacts

Relevant to the phenomenon of the *secondary impact* of missions is also the fact that the Evangelical Awakening spurred the Industrial Revolution. After years of Wesley's tireless travels, hundreds of English villages now had morally transformed people who could be trusted. So? So it was now possible for the mass production of, say, ax heads that could safely be sent to a distant village without the fear of not being paid back. England was becoming a single market. This allowed and fostered the Industrial Revolution. In the USA, a similar thing happened as the result of the Second Awakening, which elicited a listing of trustworthy people west across the Adirondacks. That project eventually became the credit rating and information corporation known as Dun and Bradstreet.

But, there was a downside. Sending mass-produced axes out to the villages of England—and other parallel things—put village workers out of work, in sort of a country-level "globalization." Those unemployed workers then gravitated to London looking for jobs (as in most of the cities of the world today) and made London a hellhole of squalor and disease. By 1850, 20% of the working men in England were too malnourished to go to work! That was enough to trigger Friedrich Engels' scholarly *The Condition of the Working Class in England in 1844*, undergirding the eruption of Communism. He was the brilliant friend of Karl Marx. Our missionaries need to be prepared to deal with secondary effects.

Another example of unwelcome secondary impact would be my own work in Guatemala. Over the years it has been a smashing success as a *spiritual* mission. But globalization has destroyed the way of life and out of sheer desperation now more than half of all fathers are illegals in this country, tearing apart hundreds of families, leaving children to grow up into drugs and gangs. But, note, "Bible and bare hands" missionaries are not likely to anticipate, much less be able to deal with, such secondary effects.

Lest we think Carey invented Protestant missions, it should be noted that flickerings of mission interest had preceded his work, e.g. the Quakers in the 1600s and the Moravians in the early 1700s. But the combination of a flood of new mission agencies, along with significant opposition to the very idea of foreign missions, had not occurred earlier in the Protestant sphere. And notice the curious coincidence, that the Carey Era of Protestant missions emerged at the very moment the economic and cultural roots of the Catholic, Continental missions were being destroyed. Yet, by 1800 the Catholic orders had planted a substantial global base of faith. Would the Protestants ever catch up? Yes, if you wait 200 years.

Struggle, Opposition, Transformation

Thus, the First Era promoted the Protestant awakening to global missions. Vigorous arguments about its validity slowed it at every step, but it at least allowed the First, William-Carey, Era to struggle into existence. Nothing spectacular. The British Methodists after 1800 sent 35 missionaries to West Africa over a period of the next 35 years. Tropical diseases meant not a single one lived more than 24 months after arrival. Yet, there were still new volunteers. No wonder they decided to ship their belongings to the field in caskets.

Early confusion about the leadership structure of missions—whether it should be the board at home or a field council—almost killed Carey's work in India, and for five years threatened Hudson Taylor's. In any case missionaries in this era mainly went to the coastlands. Inland territories, usually far more dangerous, were yet to be challenged. For many years opposition to all missions continued, not just from churchmen-theologians but from secular forces ranging from the East India Company, which rigidly excluded missionaries from its territories, to members of the British Parliament who were told that

> The sending of missionaries into our Eastern possessions is the maddest, most extravagant, most costly, most indefensible project which has ever been suggested by a moonstruck fanatic. Such a scheme is pernicious, imprudent, useless, harmful, dangerous, profitless, fantastic. It strikes against all reason and sound policy. It brings the peace and safety of our possessions into peril. (Google "moonstruck fanatic")

However, by 1813 Evangelicals in Parliament were able to force the East India Company to allow at least *English* missionaries into India.

Soon after 1800, two momentous events took place. As Americans had expected and dreaded ever since the close of the Revolutionary War, the British reappeared in force in 1812. Secondly, new and profound awakenings began to take place throughout the new Atlantic-bound republic. Also in 1812, as mentioned, the American Board of Commissioners for Foreign Missions was founded. Then, the British, partly due to their preoccupation with Napoleon at Waterloo, abruptly gave up their War of 1812 against the new American republic, signing the Treaty of Ghent in 1815. That astounding and unexpected event, plus the incredible Louisiana Purchase, threw open the whole North American continent for occupation (ignoring the rights of the Native Americans) and as a result, one of history's greatest migrations fairly exploded into existence as Americans moved west in thousands of "Conestoga wagons" to start a new life. That massive development provided the kind of social upheaval that often supports religious awakenings and mission thinking.

Thus, the Second Great Awakening burgeoned into full force in the period between the end of the War of 1812 (1815) and the beginning of the Civil War (1861). Between these two wars extensive religious awakenings, coupled with the general upheaval, *fostered the most extensive positive transformation any country has ever experienced in history*. At the same time, this transformation demonstrated the continuing force of the earlier Evangelical Awakening which had already highlighted a strong emphasis on both evangelism and social reform, Kingdom Mission at its best.

The resulting transformation of the young nation was so extensive we sometimes read back into the ethos of our earlier Founding Fathers the bold and creative Christian character of this later, much more Christian, period. Politicians, wealthy families, and commercial leaders created many reforming societies. Examples include the American Tract Society, the American Seamen's Friend Society and societies for the abolition of slavery. Alexis de Tocqueville back then, and secular historians to this day, have been so impressed by the creative social vigor in this period that many speak of an "Evangelical Empire" in that period. Charles Finney, an attorney turned revivalist, is the most prominent such symbol. But there were also thousands of others, including the pastor Sylvester Graham who went about preaching against the use of white flour in favor of God's whole-wheat flour resulting in Graham flour and Graham crackers. "Johnny Appleseed" blanketed whole states with his seeds. All this was an impressive and God-glorifying aspect of Kingdom Mission.

Creativity, Good and Not So Good
This awakening also involved religious creativity, both positive and negative, typical of the mission field today. William Miller led tens of thousands standing out on housetops to expect Christ's imminent return. Joseph Smith led tens of thousands to believe God was calling out "Latter-Day Saints." Mary Baker Patterson Glover Eddy invented Christian Science with her book *Science and Health with Key to the Scriptures*. The Shakers built buildings with perfection and prohibited marriage. In the Oneida Community everyone married everyone. In a different category, Mary Ellen White almost singlehandedly created the Seventh-Day Adventist tradition. Even the Presbyterians argued over denominational vs. interdenominational mission agencies and other things and split their entire denomination in 1837 when 1210 ministers were able to vote 1200 others out.

Yes, we need soberly to expect this kind of diversity overseas when spiritual revival occurs. For example, thousands of diverse, African-led semi-Christian movements already exist (perhaps 70 million people in 20,000 movements?). In China, secondary effects resulting from the missionary-indoctrinated Hong Xiuquan (who eventually felt he was God's Other Son) included the Taiping movement (often called a *rebellion*). Hong produced a huge "God Worshippers" subset of the country, which opposed the supposed illegitimate authority of the Manchus—somewhat like the American rebels in the American Revolution, or the Southern "Rebels" in the Civil War. While Hong's movement was highly spiritual, Bible-emphasizing and reforming, it was unbalanced, and was finally put down by the Manchus with the essential military aid of the British and French. *Perhaps 30 million died in the process!* Is this why the Chinese are still wary of the power of Christian movements?

Kingdom Mission?

As is readily noticeable, this period displayed in general a distinctly novel Christianity that emphasized getting people forgiven and to heaven, but in the meantime also getting them into physical health and social reform. Within the mainline church traditions much of the texture of those times has now been lost. Traditions having European roots continued to be flooded by European immigrants of the same traditions, who were puzzled and even repulsed by the novel new perspectives engendered by the pervasive Second Awakening. Alcohol, for example, by 1850 in America was almost everywhere considered a personal and social vice. By contrast, brewing whisky was a way of life to Presbyterians back in Scotland.

However, two movements unassaulted by masses of reluctant immigrants were minted in America, the Mormons and the Seventh-Day Adventists. They retain to this day many of the novel characteristics of the general Evangelical movement in this transformative period. Those characteristics include a strong concern for world mission as well as a religious, theological and missiological concern for diet and health, to the exclusion of tea, coffee, wine and liquor—attitudes that, hard to believe, were general Evangelical traits at the time these two otherwise unrelated traditions split off from mainstream society. Today, in Mormon Utah, more pills (medical and nutritional) are produced in St.

George than any other city of America. One company alone manufactures 350 million pills per month. Similarly millions today eat Kellogg's cold cereals and value vitamins, not realizing that Adventist thinkers developed both. Nothing today compares to the quality and number of Adventist hospitals around the world.

Missions and "manifest destiny," as in earlier global European expansion, were closely tied together. Reminiscent of the Crusades, many Americans understood the Kingdom of God to include a spiritual and military manifest destiny to seize Texas and California from Mexico, and a little later to exclude the British from the Northwest by suddenly pushing the Canadian-American border out to the Pacific. Not stopping there, they seized the mission-transformed Sandwich Islands (now Hawaii), Western Samoa, Guam, Puerto Rico and the Philippines. Missions and manifest destiny, as in earlier global European expansion, were closely tied together. In the case of the Philippines it became ours (only after an incredible blood bath, mainly unreported) because President McKinley had knelt in prayer seeking God's will for the "benighted" Filipinos just then struggling out from under Mexican control. Meanwhile, California enacted a statute guaranteeing a sizeable bounty for anyone bringing in the ears or the scalp of an Indian. This appalling law was on the books for 50 years, from 1852 to 1902. (Does that sound like East Africa Christian Hutus in 1994 chopping up hundreds of thousands of Tutsis?). It was, in any case, a shocking contrast to the patient, if somewhat ineffective, decades of work by Franciscans among the Native Americans in California. These American "crusades" were, like the classical Crusades, uneasy mixtures of high-minded religion, low-born politics, and military violence.

The immense religious optimism and expansive visions of the 1815-1860 period were not entirely extinguished by the Civil War, even though that war was one of history's most tragic and destructive. (There were forty times as many deaths in the suppression of the Taiping movement in China, which ended at about the same time.) Like the Revolutionary War, the Civil War was created and supported to some great extent by the depth of sincerity of revival-energized people on both sides. Had General Lee not sensed Lincoln's lavish generosity behind Grant's offers at the Appomattox truce he would not have urged the other Southern generals to give up the fight, and guerrilla warfare would have dragged on for years. Curiously, some scholars see a significant achievement of the war in the fact that before the war both the Northern and Southern states were by no means unified much less brilliantly conscious of being part of a nation state. But, the war unified the Northern states and, separately, unified the Southern states as never before, and the truce at Appomattox then "created" a single country where in many ways none had viably existed before.

More for our concern here, the war killed off so many men, from teens on up, that women were both allowed and even forced to take over the running of farms, banks and businesses and even to found their own colleges. Most of today's elite women's colleges, Bryn Mawr, Wellesley, Vassar, Radcliffe, Smith, Mt. Holyoke, Barnard, even Mills college in California, were either founded or transformed into colleges by women in the absence of men just after the Civil War, *and for the exclusive purpose of training women as foreign missionaries.* (Note that in the days prior to Hudson Taylor's "lay" mission it was often assumed that you had to be a college graduate to be a missionary—thus favoring wealthier families.) The first all-women mission board, the Women's Union Missionary Society, run by women and sending only women, was founded just before the Civil War but flourished after the war. In the next 30 years women founded 40 boards of missions to support financially and/ or to work alongside existing men-and-women denominational boards. By 1900 they had formed 180,000 congregation-based "Women's Missionary Societies" and had indirectly created the highly mission-minded Young Peoples Society of Christian Endeavor (CE) which to this day is not only the largest global Christian youth movement, but without it the much lauded Student Volunteer Movement for Foreign Missions, born in 1886, would have never gotten off the ground. By 1906 CE had 67,000 societies around the world and four million members. These movements, note, were still holistic and transformational, involving a Kingdom Mission clearly supported by Church Mission.

THE SECOND ERA: 1865–1980
Inland Territories, Loss of Kingdom Mission
As we approach the end of the 1800s, several things cry out for attention.

Gradual Reduction of Kingdom Mission
Did the high-flown optimism of the earlier revival period continue despite the horrifying setback of the Civil War and the massive immigration which tripled the U. S. population between 1850 and 1900 (and proved hard for the revival movement to digest)? Yes, in a moderated form among the wealthy few who were college educated. And there were wealthy Evangelicals. The "Gay Nineties" (1890-1899) were an incredible waste of money as families, some of them Evangelical, competed in throwing enormously expensive parties.

College students, as late as 1900, were only two percent of the population. But, the continuing, society-changing force of the earlier Evangelicalism was still expressed, for example, in that 1896 hymn, "America the Beautiful" which looked forward to a changed world in which "alabaster cities gleam undimmed by human tears." Furthermore, the Student Volunteer Movement (a college-level, generally wealthy movement of influential families) represented a carryover of this social optimism. Today, huge prestigious universities are to be found all over Asia, and in every province of China, created by the lingering force of the earlier age. Schools and universities, opposed by Carey's supporters (and some of his modern interpreters), were a considerable force in opening minds to the larger world of nature and nature's God. The Bible classes and chapels of 240 Christian schools in India are one of the major explanations for the existence of millions of believers who are still culturally Hindu.

What ever happened to this First Era "civilizing"? How did a song arise so different as "This world is not my home, I'm just-apassin' through"?

The Emergence of Church-Mission-Only

Well, more and more, due to the influence of the waves of immigration already mentioned, the Darwinian disturbance, and then destructive "higher criticism" of the Bible coming in from Germany (which carried the universities and the mainline seminaries), Evangelical leaders no longer ran the country. Nevertheless, there were the enormous counterbalancing gains in evangelism among the working class through the efforts of D. L. Moody. The latter now became the determinative force of the Christian movement in America, tipping the Gospel in favor of the simpler, less optimistic, religion of the masses. Repeated events suggested for many that belief in the imminence of the Second Coming of Christ outmoded all efforts to remake this world.

Meanwhile, in 1865, J. Hudson Taylor, heard God's call to found a mission to go to the *interior* of China. In the context of English social structure, what was regarded as his "lower-class" mission pushed inland, and so did those many other agencies that followed in its tracks, such as the Sudan Interior Mission, the African Inland Mission, the Heart of Africa Mission, and the Regions Beyond Missionary Union, etc. For many years these all constituted one of the two poles of the Second Era's polarization.

Incidentally, all these agencies followed Taylor's "Faith Principle," each individual missionary family waiting on God to provide, not on a salary from their mission board. These agencies came to be called "the faith missions," even though they were more significantly characterized by their endeavor to go to the inland frontiers.

Unlike Carey, Taylor's emphasis was not on *whether* to go or not, but *where* to go. More specifically, Taylor's task was the Pioneer and Paternal stages of *early, new* mission work, in contrast to the *later* Partnership and Participation stages of missiological perspective of those working in *advanced* fields. Taylor's concern, in further contrast, was that missionaries to China ought *only* to evangelize as they went deliberately beyond the coastlands. The Sandwich Islands (Hawaii), for example, unlike China's interior, was an *advanced* field and, as such, the missionaries after many decades of successful work decided it was time to *go home*—at about the time Taylor's mission was *going out!*

This was in a way a polarization. One pole was the civilizing *and* evangelizing perspective of the leaders of the First Era—of William Carey plus the many who had read and yielded to his immensely influential little book *An Enquiry into the Obligation of Christians to Use Means for the Conversion of the Heathens.* The other pole was those like Taylor who felt the call to start from scratch beyond the coastlands—with working-class missionaries, *emphasizing only evangelism.* Interestingly, it may have been one result of Taylor's deep faith and fervent prayers that after twenty years God sent the sparsely educated D.L. Moody to win seven aristocrats in England, mainly from the Cambridge student body, revered athletes including C. T. Studd, the English Michael Jordan of cricketers, to join Taylor and eventually lift his struggling mission into upper-class ranks, well-deserved fame and a larger-than-pure-proclamation approach.

Note that the so-called "Negro Spirituals," being the work of disempowered people, talk of heaven rather than social action. Something similar was true for the missions of working-class people. College in 1900, remember, was for the wealthy two percent. Typical of the missions representing non-college people was, understandably, an absence of any great reflection on the overhaul of society—as with the themes of the "Negro Spirituals." Taylor is known for his at-least-logical idea that if a thousand missionaries would evangelize 50 Chinese per day for a thousand days, all of China would be evangelized. [This was based on the assumption that there were 50 million people in China which may have been true as late as 1500 AD. But in Taylor's day, even after the incredible devastation of the Taiping war, there were probably more like 400 million. But the sweeping idea is clear.]

The point is that other missionaries in China, like the theological college graduate, Timothy Richard, a British Baptist missionary, were trying to produce an entirely new educational system on the national level. And of course, Taylor's own mission would soon be taken over by college people with eventually a broader vision and greater social influence. Yet, both missionaries had an incredible impact on the history of China.

Yes, Taylor's people, who in the early period were advised not to linger long enough to plant churches, finally slowed down long enough to do so. But they still did not think a lot about reforming society. At the very time that Taylor was greatly expanding his superb mission in China on the sole basis of evangelism, other missionaries were working to establish universities and to affect the educational system. This they finally did with enduring success. This polarization would characterize much of the next (20th) century.

Class Divergence Sets In
A carryover of the 19th century, college-type "civilizing" mission strategy is seen substantially in the Student Volunteer Movement for Foreign Missions (SVM), which continued into the early 20th century. The word *student* in the title of the SVM meant *college* student, not *Bible Institute* student, even though 157 Bible Institutes would produce many missionaries and become colleges by the end of the 20th century. Yet, as late as 1925, 75% of

American missionaries were sent out by the mainline churches, and were virtually all college people.

At the same time, something like class divergence was going on as the bulk of Evangelicals swelled to constitute millions of non-college, working-class masses which championed Moody more than Wilberforce or even Wesley. The latter's social reform activities were remembered only vaguely, if at all.

In this polarization, one pole was represented by the college-level Student Volunteers, who still thought in terms of establishing universities on the field and glorifying God by tackling the broader issues of the Kingdom of God—*Kingdom Mission*. The other pole thought in terms of glorifying God by establishing Bible schools and extending personal salvation—*Church Mission*. This was the polarization of the Second Era. There was not yet an absence of evangelism at either pole.

The one group would organize the Ecumenical Missionary Conference of 1900 in New York's Carnegie Hall, with President McKinley giving the opening address. This group would support the great Edinburgh 1910 conference, the later International Missionary Council and eventually the World Council of Churches.

Living in the overlap of the Second and Third Eras, two of the college type Student Volunteers were William Cameron Townsend, who made tribal challenges famous in the founding of Wycliffe Bible Translators, and Donald Anderson McGavran, who made everyone aware of the challenge of socially distinct (caste) groups through the Fuller School of World Mission, which he founded. Both men, though college people, appealed successfully to the mass of generally non-college Evangelicals, but especially to those toward the end of the 20th century who were increasingly college graduates.

Both men personally believed decidedly in Kingdom Mission. Townsend, for example, won over the President of Mexico by assisting a village of Indians to grow vegetables. His willingness to cooperate with Catholics took Wycliffe Bible Translators out of the Interdenominational Foreign Mission Association.

The more "conservative" Church Mission group included large minorities of Evangelicals within the mainline denominations, plus an increasing number of small, distinctly Evangelical denominations and many independent congregations, as well as the growing number of Pentecostal groups. This sphere was either oblivious to, or definitely opposed to, the level of social concern of the older denominations. Meanwhile, the limited influence of Evangelicals in the professions, universities and civil governments in the United States tended to prevent these Evangelicals from spawning expansive ideas about changing this world.

Alternatively, they developed detailed concepts of Biblical prophecy, the "end times," the return of Christ, and the Millennium, and tended to de-emphasize, almost to the point of total exclusion, ideas of social reform. Among them even the word *Kingdom* was for years suspect as evidence of "liberal" thinking. *Yet, they were conscientiously active in what was within their power to do*: inner-city missions, for example. Their missionaries on the field did a huge amount of what they could, without expansive plans, to relieve suffering and sickness, but held as highest priority the founding of Bible institutes and personal, not so much social, salvation.

Even the "mainline" sphere became deeply influenced by the Evangelicals within their membership, due in part to Evangelical donor perspectives. They were pressured essentially, like political candidates today, to speak the Evangelical language. Simultaneously, another reason for the growing influence of non-college Evangelicals was because more and more of the children of these Evangelicals were going to universities and the 157 Bible Institutes were themselves morphing into Bible Colleges, into standard liberal arts colleges and into universities.

Secular Events Confirm Pessimism

But note, the first half of the 20th century confronted both groups with massive setbacks. Tragic events tended to justify the concentration on heaven, and encouraged a widespread replacement of optimism about this world with deep pessimism and rapture thinking.

The 20th century began with the deadly Boxer Rebellion in China in 1900, which gruesomely murdered scores of missionaries and many other foreigners. Ironically, the triumphalistic Ecumenical Missionary Conference in New York was held a month earlier. Neither that huge conference nor the Welsh Revival of 1910 nor the Edinburgh World Missionary Conference of 1910 could entirely offset the implications of the setback in China.

There was also the sinking of the Titanic in 1912, which symbolized the sinking of confidence in human engineering achievements. Then the 1st World War struck and the often forgotten global flu pandemic killed more than fifty million people (2.5 to 5 percent of global population). The insane "Roaring Twenties" collapsed in the panic of 1929, ushering in the years of deep and painful global financial depression. Struggling out of that then took the whole world into the jaws of the 2nd World War—which did one good thing, by treating over ten million American soldiers to a world tour and as a result generated 150 new mission agencies in the first five years after the war's end.

By this time the theology of both poles had been affected. All these tragedies seemed to confirm the Bible Institute people's pessimism about any kind of earthly Kingdom of God. But even mainline theologians in the tradition of the Student Volunteer Movement developed theologies explaining and expecting failure in mission. John R. Mott's final statement at the World Missionary Conference of 1910 had been "now begins the conquest," but this was soon considered an embarrassingly imperialistic form of "triumphalism." While in 1925, as mentioned, the missionaries who were being sent out by the mainline denominations still constituted 75% of the total from America, by 1975 they were less than 5% of the total. The concept of Kingdom Mission was dead or dying.

However, it must be said that the drop-off in missionary sending in the mainline denominations was not merely the child of theological pessimism or liberalism. It also resulted from the fact that the goal of mission for them had gradually become redefined as merely Church Mission, church planting. The (mainly Evangelical) missionaries within the older denominations had by this time accordingly developed movements with field memberships running into the hundreds of thousands. Under the circumstances, sending more missionaries to those fields virtually implied (and would still imply) the rewording of the Great Commission into "Go ye into all the world and meddle in the national churches."

THE THIRD ERA: 1935 TO PRESENT
Unreached Peoples, Recovery of Kingdom Mission
Meanwhile those two young men of the college-level Student Volunteer Movement, Cameron Townsend and Donald McGavran, began to be noticed. Townsend was in so much of a hurry to get to the mission field that he didn't bother to finish college. Although he helped initiate the Third Era, he went to Guatemala as a Second Era missionary, building on work which had been done in the past. In Guatemala, as in all other mission fields, there was plenty to do for missionaries working with established national churches.

Townsend
But Townsend was alert enough to notice (and it was pointed out by more-experienced missionaries already working in the Indian languages) that the majority of Guatemala's population

did not speak Spanish. As he moved from village to village, trying to distribute scriptures written in the Spanish language, he finally yielded to the fact that Spanish evangelism could never reach most of Guatemala's predominantly indigenous citizens. He was further convinced of this when, legend has it, an Indian leader asked him, "If your God is so smart, why can't He speak our language?" He was befriended by a group of older missionaries who had already concluded that the indigenous populations needed to be reached in their own languages. He was just 23 when he began to move on the basis of this new perspective. No one could have predicted the spectacular results.

Surely Cameron Townsend is comparable to William Carey and Hudson Taylor. Like them, Townsend saw that there were still unreached frontiers, and for almost a half century he waved the flag for the by-passed and overlooked tribal peoples of the world. He started out hoping to encourage older boards to reach out to tribal peoples. Like Carey and Taylor, he ended up (in 1934) starting his own mission agency, later called Wycliffe Bible Translators, which was dedicated to teaching linguistics as a prime tool for reaching these new frontiers. At first he thought there must be about 500 unreached tribal groups in the world. (He was extrapolating from the large number of tribal languages in Mexico alone). Later, he revised his figure to 1,000, then 2,000, and now it is over 5,000. As his conception of the enormity of the task increased, the size of his organization increased, numbering over 6,000 adult workers by 2008.

McGavran

As Townsend was ruminating in Guatemala, Donald McGavran was beginning to yield to the seriousness, not of linguistic barriers, but of India's amazing social and cultural barriers. Townsend discerned and promoted the reality of linguistically diverse (and overlooked) tribes; McGavran highlighted and promoted the social and cultural diversity of a more nearly universal category he labeled "homogeneous units" which today are more often called "people groups." Paul Hiebert, missionary anthropologist, employed the terminology of "horizontal segmentation" for the tribes, where each occupies its own turf, and "vertical segmentation" for groups distinguished not by geography but by rigid social or cultural differences. McGavran's terminology described both kinds even though he was mainly thinking about the more subtle vertical segmentation characteristic of India.

Once such a social group is penetrated by diligently taking advantage of a missiological breakthrough along social lines, McGavran's strategic concept, already mentioned, of a "Bridge of God" to that people group comes into the picture. The corollary of this truth is the fact that, *until* such a breakthrough is made, normal evangelism and church planting cannot begin.

McGavran did not found a new mission (Townsend did so, remember, only when existing missions did not adequately respond to the tribal challenge). But McGavran built the largest school of mission in the world and his active efforts and writings spawned both the Church Growth Movement and indirectly the Frontier Mission movement. The former is devoted to expanding within already penetrated groups. The latter (which he did not agree with until his last few years) is devoted to deliberately approaching the remaining totally unpenetrated groups.

Edinburgh 1980, Turning Point

As with Taylor before them, for twenty years Townsend and McGavran attracted little attention. But by the 1950s both had wide audiences. In 1980, 46 years after Townsend's 1934 organizational move, a 1910-like conference was held, consisting exclusively of mission leaders and focusing precisely on both kinds of forgotten groups which these two men had emphasized. The Edinburgh-1980 World Consultation on Frontier Missions was at that date the largest mission meeting in history, if measured by the number of mission agencies sending delegates.

And, wonder of wonders, 57 Third World agencies, fully a third, sent delegates. (None were at the 1910 meeting.) This meeting, though not widely noticed, was crucial to the Third Era, planting Unreached Peoples vision throughout the world. It also included a concurrent youth meeting, the International Student Consultation on Frontier Missions, pointing up for all future mission meetings an "intergenerational" ideal—*to include significant youth participation.* The student group started in 1983 the *International Journal of Frontier Missiology* (all of its hundreds of keen articles are all available on the web, at www.ijfm.org).

As happened in the early stages of the first two eras, the Third Era has spawned a number of new mission agencies. Some, like the New Tribes Mission, carry in their names reference to this new emphasis. The names of others, such as Gospel Recordings and Mission Aviation Fellowship, refer to the new technologies necessary for the reaching of tribal and other isolated peoples of the world. Some Second Era agencies, like SIM International, have never ceased to stress frontiers and have merely increased their staff so they can penetrate further—to people groups previously overlooked.

More recently many have begun to realize that tribal peoples are not the only forgotten peoples. Many other groups, some even in the middle of partially Christianized areas, have been completely overlooked. These peoples, including overlooked tribals, have come to be called "Unreached Peoples" and are defined by ethnic or sociological traits. They are peoples so different from the cultural traditions of any existing congregation that specifically cross-cultural *mission* strategies (rather than ordinary *evangelistic* techniques) are necessary to achieve the "missiological breakthrough" essential to planting truly indigenous beachheads of faith within their particular cultural traditions.

Polarization Growing and Decreasing

But the irony is that at a time when missions of the older denominations were in decline—considerably due to a longstanding aversion by the mass of Evangelicals to the "non-evangelistic" activities of those mainline missions—the "true" Evangelical missions that were taking their place were themselves becoming inhabited by university people gaining an equivalent increase of awareness of the larger dimensions of the Gospel—and "non evangelistic" activities.

A true recovery on the part of Evangelical missions from their earlier evangelistic narrowness is even more significantly portrayed, unexpectedly, by the giving patterns of donors and the interests of young people. In a recent five-year period in this century, U. S. church-planting missions grew 2.7% while Evangelical relief and development agencies grew 74.8%. Yet, this divergence between the two groups must be considered an unwelcome continuation of the Second Era polarization.

Thus the Third Era has seen the adoption of a new and more precise definition of the *ethne*, the *nations* of the Bible, and effectively defined those peoples that are still unengaged by missionary outreach as of highest priority. It also displayed a steady, if very gradual, recovery from a rich but narrow emphasis on heaven that had replaced the 19th century merger of heaven and earth in mission purpose. In neither case—Unreached Peoples or Kingdom Mission—is the Third Era finished. Arguments and confusion still exist over the present significance of remaining small peoples, as well as over the full meaning of "Thy Kingdom come, Thy will be done on earth as it is in heaven."

This latter "kingdom" confusion is more complex than the Unreached Peoples challenge. The lingering terror and fear that arise in some circles when there is any talk of seeking to extend the Kingdom of God in this world is in good part the result of the bitter, lengthy "Fundamentalist/Modernist" controversies which dominated much of the first half of the 20th century. Are we going to fall into that again?

That polarization is by no means dead, if only because, as fast as many Evangelicals gain influence in society, upgrade their general education and missiology, and become able to entertain more expansive plans to promote the growth of the Church and the Kingdom of God, other thousands are just coming into faith and typically yearn for simple answers. This recalls the Jesus Movement of the early 1970s that swept many into an earnestly pursued but simplistic theology which, for example, acknowledged only one specific translation of the Bible (NASB) to be trustworthy. In fact, as late as 1973 about one twentieth of the congregations of the Presbyterians in the South withdrew to form a new denomination. This reflected the polarization we have been describing as well as the social levels of small, rural churches and city churches.

Is there really a massive transition that explains the polarization? George Marsden, an eminent historian of American Christianity, may have only partially overstated it when he said,

> These American Christians underwent a remarkable transformation in their relationship to the culture. Respectable "evangelicals" in the 1870s, by the 1920s they had become a laughingstock, ideological strangers in their own land.

Now 100 years later, James Beverley, a professor at the Tyndale University in Toronto, Canada, states:

> Are leaders in the Charismatic world going to curb the seeming obsession with angels, trips to heaven, gold dust, feathers from heaven, heavenly oil, heavenly gems, gold fillings and out-of-body travel? Lee Grady, editor of *Charisma* Magazine, has critiqued Bentley on these kinds of issues, especially for his incredible reports about angels and his wild stories about his regular trips to heaven. Sadly, Grady received a lot of condemnation from other leaders...

You can be sure that there are not a lot of well-to-do university graduates in Todd Bentley's audience. In any case, missionaries need to expect things like this more often in the non-Western world than they occur here.

But to understand the durability of the social cleavage underlying the polarization being described, it is only necessary to realize that, over the decades, in meetings of the American Society of Missiology (ASM) and the Evangelical Missiological Society (EMS) there is never any reference to each other. Dr. George Peters of Dallas Theological Seminary and myself from Fuller Theological Seminary headed up a side meeting at the huge IFMA/EFMA (see below) "Greenlake 1971" Conference on Church-Mission Relations, and recruited 65 to be founding members of the American Society of Missiology in 1972.

Thus the ASM has from the start been virtually dominated by "Evangelicals." However, as intended, other people recruited other members from "mainline" spheres, both Catholic and Protestant, often from theological seminaries. That inclusivity of the ASM provided rationale for a separate society (EMS) made up of mainly professors of Bible Institutes/Colleges or schools that were once in that category. Yet many Evangelical professors are members of both the ASM and the EMS, while the two societies are durably separate.

Early in the 1900s Evangelicals founded Bible Institutes rather than colleges and seminaries. But one significant seminary was established, Dallas Theological Seminary. However, it waited sixty years before joining the Association of Theological Schools.

Similarly, the National Association of Evangelicals (NAE), founded in 1945, was a counterpart to the National Council of Churches of Christ in the USA (NCCCUSA), while the Evangelical Foreign Missions Association (EFMA affiliated with the NAE, and recently renamed The Mission Exchange) was a counterpart to the NCCCUSA's Division of Overseas Ministries

(DOM). Mainline denominational mission agencies of the DOM don't join the EFMA, nor do the denominational agencies of the EFMA join the DOM. Yet Evangelicals individuals in substantial numbers are to be found within both the DOM and the EFMA. Attitudes have changed faster than institutions.

But What Is the Gospel of the Kingdom?

Curiously (and granted that very few people think this way today) neither of the two poles—neither the influential Student Volunteers nor the heaven-and-personal-salvation oriented Bible Institute people—have had a very well-defined concept of a Gospel of the Kingdom which would see the 40-hour week of lay people (beyond evangelism on the job) as a sacred calling. Could not lay people deliberately choose a different career based not on its salary level but on its strategic contribution to the will of God on earth? Many urgent problems and evils still cry out for solution, but are often totally outside of the theological box of those who are content with Church Mission. Sadly, the goal of planting the Church in every people group, of merely extending Christianity, whether in the USA or around the world, is the most common understanding of the extent of God's purpose in our world. There is little room for a concept, apart from professional, church-related ministry, of a "full-time Christian."

But when every believer is expected to be consciously and deliberately "in mission," does that then mean nothing is mission? No, it just means that there are different types of mission. There will always be the fearsomely difficult cross-cultural pioneer mission. But those of us who have been championing that as the highest priority have no power to reserve the word *mission* for that urgent type of mission.

We now have a better understanding of the earlier, somewhat artificial, and damaging, polarization between Church Mission and Kingdom Mission. We don't need to be forever defeated by pendulum swings between the two poles. Today most of the sons and daughters of Moody's converts are now influential middle-class people such that college people are now no longer a tiny upper-class minority. Today, those tempted to glory in an artificially simple approach to the Bible and missions are mainly either a fundamentalist residue or a brand new hyper-charismatic fringe.

An optimistic case study in this Third Era would be to note the excellent headway being made by mission thinkers and agencies today in what is called "The Insider Approach" to Muslims, Hindus, and Buddhists, with whom missions have made little progress in times past.

Lately it is being realized that Paul's example (permitting Greeks to continue to be Greeks as they followed Christ) is parallel to allowing Muslims, Hindus, and Buddhists to retain much of their language and culture as Christ's followers. That significant phenomenon is dealt with elsewhere in this course.

Conclusion: How Far Have We Come?

We need to recognize the impetus toward the recovery of full-blown Kingdom Mission in the writings of three men. Some people insist they were early prophets of a Fourth Era, for better or worse. Professor Carl F. H. Henry in 1947 came out with his historic *The Uneasy Conscience of Modern Fundamentalism*. In 1957 Professor Timothy Smith produced his pivotal *Revivalism and Social Reform*, unearthing the impact on society of the Second Awakening in the first half of the 19th Century. Finally, Professor David O. Moberg in 1967 gave us his book entitled *The Great Reversal* (released later in various versions), which detailed the decline from what we call Kingdom Mission (going beyond personal transformation) to a focus on the personal within what here is called Church Mission.

For the average lay person, Church Mission, the mission to promote and extend the Church as an institution, is described as the "pray and give type of "after-hours" Christianity." Church

Mission together with Kingdom Mission should be a 24/7 "full-time Christian" type of Christianity. What does "full-time Christian" mean? It means that the mission to promote the Kingdom, or Kingdom Mission, involves or should involve every move a lay person makes in his forty-hour week of work *in addition to what he may do for the church* "after hours" in Church Mission. Examples might be teaching first grade as a holy calling, working at any legitimate work as a holy calling but being alert to the opportunity to pursue a career to end global human slavery, or extreme poverty, etc. That is what would be a "Full-time Christian." It would include, of course, what we call full-time Christian service if that is the most strategic option available.

Many pastors call for people not only to believe, but to be willing to "serve Jesus Christ." However, they may mean teach Sunday School, help in the nursery, usher in church services, or support missionaries. Many pastors may even urge their people to go out in the world and do good, as individuals, but they may not be thinking of the need for church people to support and/or form serious, large agencies that are tackling the major evils, obscenities, and tragedies of this world. For them, to promote either the Kingdom of God or the Church is essentially the same thing. The Lord's Prayer then becomes too often "*Our* kingdom come" as the Church is concerned with the personal and spiritual fulfillment of its individual members, its building plans, etc., not the solution of problems beyond its boundaries.

How Far to Go?

One of the most difficult things for some people to understand is why it is impossible, not just unwise, to think of words and deeds as being separable. The Bible as God's Word would be little more than dreamy philosophy if it did not refer almost constantly to the deeds of God, the deeds of key human followers, and the deeds of His Son. In the same way, our missionary outreach must be filled with meaningful deeds or our words run thin and we do not reveal the character of God. The World Evangelical Alliance speaks discerningly of:

> Integral Mission or holistic transformation [as] the proclamation and demonstration of the gospel. It is not simply that evangelism and social action are to be done alongside each other.

They are not two different things. Note that "holistic" here does not merely mean the whole man but the whole of society, the whole of this world.

Furthermore, Evangelicals today, now with far greater wealth and influence, need to realize that heightened privilege calls for expanded and more complex responsibility. The amount of money Bill and Melinda Gates are putting into the defeat of malaria is no more than peanuts compared to the funds Evangelicals annually fritter away on nonessentials. Yet no respectable, organized effort of Evangelicals now exists that is stepping up to bat to seek the eradication of diseases that afflict millions, including millions of Christians. Does the conventional message of churches today challenge followers of Christ to deliberately choose microbiology as well as "Christian ministry"? (Note that Kingdom Mission means more than "*social* action" if it is to eradicate disease germs. The Bible speaks of *restoration* not just *social* action.) Come on! Can't we digest the fact that thousands and thousands of Christian families around the world are, right now, so poor and diseased that when they can't feed their children they must sell them into forced labor for them to be able to eat? In Pakistan hundreds of thousands fall into this category. Half of such children die by age 12.

Doing lots of good things, or as someone has said, "Keepin' busy for Jesus" individually maybe a case of "good but not good enough." Our Evangelical perspective has become so individualized that we may only think of individual good works. Doing good little things wherever convenient may sometimes be merely a way to justify and make credible in our own eyes our minimal personal salvation. Starting with our own talents and interests is common but is the way of the world—it is getting things backwards. Don't be upset—this is going upstream—but how can one's subjective personal interests accurately predict God's priorities?

We must start with *His concerns,* whatever our gifts, wants, and abilities. How can the four-year college major we once chose without reflecting on God's priorities be assumed to define the direction of the next 50 years? We must "give our utmost for His highest." Our obedience is certainly flawed if focused only on what the world approves. *Our obligation is to seek the expansion of the knowledge of the glory of God and His Kingdom, and this would logically require us each to prayerfully seek God about doing the hardest thing we are able to do in the most crucial task we can find.* First John 3:8 says, "The Son of God appeared for this purpose, that He might destroy the works of the Devil." To follow Jesus is to go to war. This side of the Millennium that's what the Christian life is. In a war *what needs to be done* comes first. And a true sense of accomplishment is not that you did what you wanted to do, or what you thought you were best at, but what you felt convinced was most crucial, most important. Doing good things is the biblical way to portray God's character and glory only if we are willing to act without inserting personal conditions.

Thus, we see that the Third Mission Era, in so far as it recognizes both Unreached Peoples and a recovering Kingdom Mission, reveals significant demands, unfailing inspiration and incredible promise.

Reprinted with permission from Winter, Ralph D. and Stephen C. Hawthorne, eds. Perspectives on the World Christian Movement: A Reader. Pasadena: William Carey Library, 2009, pp. 263-278.

MISSIO DEI

Eddie Arthur

Introduction

Missio Dei is a Latin theological term that can be translated as "Mission of God." It refers to the work of the church as being part of God's work. So the church's mission is a subset of a larger whole mission that is it is both part of God's mission to the world and not the entirety of God's work in the world.[1]

This definition provides a simple introduction to the concept of *missio Dei* which is essentially that the work or mission of the church is a subset of the work of God in the world, rather than something with an independent existence. The use of *missio Dei* has evolved considerably over the last fifty years, therefore this essay will start with a brief historical overview of the term before considering the implications and usefulness of contemporary usage, focusing (not exclusively) on the Evangelical wing of the church.[2]

History

The term *missio Dei* itself has a long history and can be traced at least as far back as Augustine.[3] It was Aquinas who first used the term to describe the activity of the triune God, the father sending

---

[1] Wikipedia: the online encyclopaedia. www.wikipedia.org
[2] In order to get an accurate picture of the development of the theology of *missio Dei*, we will need to consider the work of some authors who use the concept without having recourse to Latin terminology.
[3] Engelsviken p.482

the Son and the Son sending the Spirit.[4] In a modern setting, Karl Barth, in a 1932 paper, set out the idea that mission was God's work and that authentic church mission must be in response to God's *missio*. This idea was picked up by Hartenstein who used the term *missio Dei* to distinguish it from the *missio ecclesiae*, the mission of the church.[5] However, it was at the 1952 Willingen meeting of the International Missionary Council that the concept of *missio Dei* was fleshed out in detail. The term *missio Dei* was not actually used at the Willingen meeting though it was used by Hartenstein[6] in his summary of the conference.

Willingen

The meeting at Willingen in Germany took place at a difficult time in the life of the Church. The Second World War had been replaced by the cold war and the church was coming to terms with the expulsion of missionaries from China.[7] Against this pessimistic background Willingen fleshed out the theology of mission that Barth, Hartenstein and others had been moving towards. In his report of the conference Hartenstein described mission as "participation in the sending of the Son, in the *missio Dei,* with an inclusive aim of establishing the Lordship of Christ over the whole redeemed creation.[8] According to Goheen, there are two new particular emphases on missiological thinking which emerged from Willingen.

First, mission is first and foremost God's mission. The church does not have a mission of its own. Rather, the primary emphasis is on what God is doing for the redemption of the world. Thereafter, consideration is given to how the church participates

---

[4] Hoffmeyer
[5] Bevans and Schroeder p.290
[6] Engelsviken p.482
[7] Bosch p.370
[8] Engelsviken p.482

in God's redeeming mission. Second, God's mission is defined in terms of the Triune character and work of God.[9]

The Trinitarian emphasis was particularly important. "Mission was understood as being derived from the very nature of God. It was thus put in the context of the doctrine of the Trinity, not of ecclesiology or soteriology."[10] Engelsviken suggests that this emphasis on a Trinitarian basis for mission is a more important outcome from Willingen than "the somewhat ambiguous phrase *missio Dei.*"[11] While there was substantial agreement on the use of terminology and the Trinitarian nature of mission, the Willingen participants were unable to agree on the extent of God's mission and the Church's role within it.

Post-Willingen

> In Willingen and period following, two major—and somewhat competing—approaches to missio Dei emerged. The first one, a dominant view in the Willingen meeting, understood mission as God's evangelizing action through the church. The second, which raised serious opposition to the dominant Willingen view was developed later... It conceived missio Dei as God's activity in the secular world over and above the church, saying, "the world provides the agenda."[12]

Goheen defines these two points of view as Christocentric-Trinitarian and Cosmocentric-Trinitarian.[13] (Philip[14] uses the terms church-centric and world-centric). The Christocentric sees God's mission as centering on the work of Christ through the Church, whereas the Cosmocentric view (of which the Dutch missiologist Hoekendijk was the most prominent proponent) sees God's mission as being active in all of the cosmos. For

---

[9] Goheen p.117
[10] Bosch p.390
[11] Engelsviken p.482
[12] Pachuau
[13] Goheen p.117
[14] Philip ch.5

Hoekendijk, the church is an appendix[15] to God's work. "When one desires to speak about God's dealings with the world, the church can be mentioned only in passing and without strong emphasis."[16] For Hoekendijk, God is at work in the world which then has an effect on the church, as opposed to the classical view which saw God at work in the church and through the church to the wider world.[17] The stress on God's mission through the wider world and not just the church was such that Newbigin could write that "Mao's *Little Red Book* became almost a new Bible.[18]

Through the 1960s an increasing number of people from a variety of confessional backgrounds adopted Hoekendijk's views[19] to such an extent that at the 1968 Uppsala conference of the WCC "the church was often ridiculed and ... the church itself was seen as an arena for mission."[20] "By consequence, evangelism practically disappeared from the mission agenda of mainline churches in the West and North."[21]

Through the decade of the 1960s there was an increasing polarization between those who took opposing views of the role of the Church in mission. Broadly speaking, Evangelicals continued to believe in a dynamic role for the church in mission, whereas those with an ecumenical perspective tended to follow Hoekendijk's Cosmocentric model. This difference in views led to a split "between the evangelical churches and the ecumenically aligned churches and organizations and thus to one of the biggest polarization processes in the church in the west since the Second World War."[22] One consequence of this split was the

---

[15] Sundermeier p.560
[16] Quoted in Engelsviken p.488
[17] Engelsviken p.489
[18] Newbigin p.18
[19] Richebacher, p.592
[20] Bevans and Schroeder p.291
[21] Matthey
[22] Richebacher p.594

establishment of the evangelical Lausanne movement as a counterpoint to the World Council of Churches.[23]

Today

In the intervening years, new insights have been read into the concept of *missio Dei,* leading to a slight blurring of the extremes of interpretation. However, these two broad understandings of *missio Dei*—Christocentric and Cosmocentric—can still be discerned in the literature. For this reason we will examine the way in which the different views of *missio Dei* have an impact on teaching about the Kingdom of God, the Church and other religions.

Missio Dei and the Kingdom of God

Videcom published a book entitled *Missio Dei* in 1965; in this book he closely tied *missio Dei* to the Kingdom of God. However, Videcom used Kingdom of God in two distinct ways: the rule of God over the whole of creation and the restoration of relationships with God and humanity through the death of Christ. This inconsistency facilitated[24] the divergence in understanding of *missio Dei* which developed during the 1960s.

If the Kingdom of God is seen as being God's rule over the whole of creation, then its realization is primarily in terms of social and ethical transformation. This view sees the advancement of the Kingdom as including the whole of history with the Church as a witness or perhaps a participant in its realization. This view clearly aligns with Hoekendijk's view of *missio Dei.* The alternative view of the Kingdom acknowledges that God rules over all of history, but sees the Kingdom as specifically referring to the impact of the redemptive work of Christ. In this view, which fits a Christocentric view of *missio Dei,* the Church is the people who belong to the Kingdom and clearly must play a central role in its inauguration.

---

[23] Richebacher p.593
[24] Engelsviken p.483

Missio Dei and the Church

Historical, denominational missions were functioned as European-based national churches extending their boundaries into unreached parts of the world[25] with their own institutional expansion and survival as priority.[26] *Missio Dei* brings a correction to this view by putting God, not the church or denomination, at the centre of mission. Mission is the originator of the Church, not the other way round.[27]

As we have seen, Hoekendijk placed a strong emphasis on mission being God centered: "Church-centric missionary thinking is bound to go astray, because it revolves around an illegitimate centre."[28] This strong emphasis led to a virtual repudiation of any role for the Church in mission.

By way of contrast, Newbigin[29] suggests that the Trinitarian nature of mission implies an important role for the Church. Communication and community lies at the heart of the Trinity and therefore must lie at the heart of Trinitarian mission. The call to conversion is a call to become part of a community, the Church, and comes from that community. Others express similar thoughts: "Both the church and the mission of the church are tools of God, instruments through which God carries out this mission."[30] "Mission is thereby seen as a movement from God to the world. The church is viewed as an instrument for that mission."[31] In this view, the whole purpose of the Church is to support the *missio Dei*[32] and Church structures exist in order to serve the community in mission.[33]

---

[25] Engelsviken p.487
[26] Guder 1998 p.5
[27] Bevans and Schroeder p.298
[28] Quoted in Engelsviken p.488
[29] Newbigin p.76
[30] Quoted in Engelsviken p.482
[31] Bosch p.390
[32] Bosch p.391
[33] Bevans and Schroeder p.299

Missio Dei and Other Religions
While the Church is key to God's work in the world, *Missio Dei* teaches us that we need to see God on a broader canvas than just through the work of the church.

> Mission as missio Dei necessarily relativizes Western understanding of mission. God cannot be restricted to what has been and is happening in Western cultural Christianity. God's work is universal in its impact.[34]

Seeing God at work in a universal sense implies that Christians need to have a humble approach to other religions. For some, who adopt the cosmocentric approach to *missio Dei*, this means that they see other religions as being able to bring salvation in the same way as Christianity.[35]

> The Mission of the Church is not God's only mission. It is not even his only world-wide mission... Few of us Christians know much about God's mission in the Islamic venture, God's mission to India and nowadays to the world through the Hindu venture.[36]

Those who take the Christocentric view agree that we need to enter into humble dialogue with other faiths, however they also stress that it is important to "do justice to our Trinitarian faith" and "to point people to Christ."[37]

Evangelicals and *Missio Dei*
Missio Dei is a theology which emphasizes both the imperative for mission and the Sovereignty of God. It is surprising, therefore, that Evangelical Christians (especially those of a Reformed background) who tend to emphasize the same things, have apparently paid little attention to *missio Dei*.[38] Lee[39] says

---

[34] Guder 2000 p.20
[35] Sundermeier p.567
[36] Smith p.366
[37] Richebacher p.597
[38] Recker p.192
[39] Lee p.143

that evangelicals lag behind ecumenicals in developing a missio Dei theology, though he does not explain why that might be so. Wickeri says that conservative evangelicals' "understanding of mission is quite different to the *missio Dei*."[40] It is no surprise that when evangelicals do talk about *missio Dei*, they adopt a Christocentric view rather than follow Hoekendijk's line.[41] It could well be that the strong separatist strand which is often a feature of Evangelical life means that they are reluctant to adopt a term which is in some way 'tainted' by liberalism or secularism. The divide in Evangelical circles about the role of social action in mission also impacts their adoption of *missio Dei*. Chai says that the Evangelical mega-churches in Korea see mission purely in terms of salvation and so suggests that they do not take *missio Dei* seriously.[42] However, there is increasingly a strong Trinitarian aspect in Evangelical missiology. This is illustrated by the Iguassou declaration: "All the persons of the Godhead are active in God's redeeming mission."[43]

Trinitarian Mission

The fact that *missio Dei* is used as a term to cover such a wide range of meaning does detract from its usefulness. Kirk[44] says "*missio Dei* has been used to advance all kinds of missiological agendas." Possibly, because of the confusion which this lack of definition engenders, the term is actually used less frequently in current literature as compared to twenty or thirty years ago.[45]

There are a number of weaknesses in the cosmocentric understanding of *missio Dei*. The understanding of the Kingdom of God as covering the whole of human history does not seem to

---

[40] Wickeri p.193
[41] Engelsviken p.491
[42] Chai p.548
[43] Taylor p.17
[44] Kirk p.25
[45] Engelsviken p.490

reflect Jesus assertion that the Kingdom 'drew near' through his ministry (Mark1:15). Equally, the approach that sees other religions as being missions equivalent to the mission of the Church does not do justice to Jesus claims to uniqueness, nor the Trinitarian nature of God. However, perhaps the greatest weakness in the cosmocentric approach is the idea that God's kingdom is being inaugurated through a continual improvement in social and ethical conditions. In the 1960s against a background of technological advance and colonial-independence this may have seemed attractive. However, hindsight reveals these improvements to have been false hopes, amounting to little more than a different form of Western religious imperialism[46] which did not do justice to the Biblical narrative of fall and redemption.

Despite the breadth of interpretation applied to the term, Bosch defends the concept of *missio Dei*: "...It cannot be denied that the *missio Dei* notion has helped to articulate the conviction that neither the Church nor any other human agent can ever be considered the author or bearer of mission. Mission is, primarily and ultimately, the work of the Triune God, Creator, Redeemer and Sanctifier, for the sake of the world."[47] Kirk emphasizes the Trinitarian nature of mission. "When Christian communities speak about God, by definition they speak about Father, Son and Holy Spirit. There simply is no other God. Therefore to speak about *missio Dei* is to indicate, without any qualification, the *missio Trinitatis.*"[48]

Despite the real disagreements which continue to exist, there is, according to Kirk[49] and Richebacher[50] a degree of consensus is appearing about the theological understanding of God's mission. "During the past half a century or so, there has been a subtle, but

---

[46] Richebacher p.593
[47] Bosch p. 391
[48] Kirk p.27
[49] Kirk p.25
[50] Richebacher p.595

nevertheless decisive, shift toward understanding mission as God's mission."[51]

Placing God at the centre of mission also involves a reorientation of thinking; "a shift from church-centered mission, to a mission-centered church."[52] "The theology of mission has become missionary theology."[53] In other words, the agenda for missionary thought and action is defined by the character of God, not the activities of the Church. The implications of this in the life and practice of the Church are far reaching.

> Evangelism is God's work long before it is our work. The Father prepares the ground, the Son gives the invitation and the Spirit prompts the person to respond in repentance and faith to the good news.[54]

The Trinitarian nature of *Missio Dei* brings all three persons of the Godhead into focus in missionary theology. This has not always been the case, for example, Goheen suggests that before Willingen, Leslie Newbigin did not give any attention to the role of the Father in mission.[55]

The Father in Mission

The overwhelming motive for mission is the compassion and love of God for his creation[56] and the end point of mission is the Kingdom, the reign of God over his people. These twin themes from *missio Dei* establish the motivation and attitude of the church in mission. Motivated by God's love, the Church should not seek to dominate or impose itself upon other people or organizations and individual church groups or organizations should not seek to exercise their rights to the detriment of others

---

[51] Bosch p.389
[52] Wickeri p.187
[53] Guder 2000 p.20
[54] Kirke p.78
[55] Goheen p.129
[56] Guder 2000 p.32, Kirk p.27

or of God's mission. "God's reign cannot be reduced to a human level or made to serve human purposes."[57] The historic confusion of the Church's mission and the secular political process in Christendom is excluded by *missio Dei*. With this in mind, Wickeri raises serious questions about the alignment between the Church and the political state in the United States today, especially in the light of the war in Iraq.[58]

The triumphalism of much of the world mission movement is drawn into question in the light of *missio Dei*.[59] There is also reason to question some aspects of American managerial missiology. Though, generally, there has been a step away from the idea of Church-centric missions; groups such as AD-2000 seem to be ignoring this trend. The elaboration of measurable and achievable goals, which is part of this missiological approach, could be seen as placing human technique and measurement at the centre of mission rather than God's bigger agenda. Because God is the creator of the whole world, salvation is not limited to the salvation of souls but includes the establishment of a new heaven and a new earth.

The Son in Mission

The incarnation lies at the heart of God's mission and provides the content, model and the inspiration for the church's mission (John 20:21).

> The missio Dei has always been the Gospel, good news about God's goodness revealed in God's word through Israel's experience, leading up to its climax and culmination in Jesus Christ.[60]

The heart of the church's mission is to communicate this Gospel of Christ's incarnation, death and resurrection. But the message must be communicated in a manner which is consistent with the

---

[57] Guder 2000 p.37
[58] Wickeri p.191
[59] Wickeri p.187
[60] Guder 2000 p.47

character of Christ. The incarnation demonstrates that God's mission is not dependant on any one human culture or language.[61] Suffering, too is an intrinsic part of the *missio Dei,* rooted in the suffering of the Son. "*Missio Dei* always leads us by way of Golgotha, by the way of suffering".[62] In becoming a man, Jesus became poor and spent a lot of time with the poor, and focusing on the needs of the poor is an intrinsic part of God's purposes for the Church. Richebacher says that poverty is the most important sign of the missionary church because Jesus fulfilled his mission by becoming poor,[63] and while we may not agree that this is *the* most important sign, it is clearly an extremely important one.

The Spirit in Mission

Christ sent his Spirit to empower his church for mission and to enlighten those who are outside of the Kingdom. This means that the church must be reliant on the Spirit both for its own activities in mission and for the effect of its work. There should be no place for organization or planning which excludes the role of the Spirit.

> Mission is not just something that the church does; it is something that is done by the Spirit, who is himself the witness, who changes both the world and the church, who always goes before the church on its missionary journey.[64]

Newbigin[65] suggests that young churches, planted by missionaries from other cultures, should find their ethical guidance from the Spirit rather than from the teaching or mores of the missionaries. In this way, the Gospel will have an authentic encounter with the new culture and allow the development of

---

[61] Guder 2000 p.78
[62] Suess p. 558
[63] Richebacher p. 594
[64] Newbigin p.57
[65] Newbigin p.132

locally relevant Christian traditions and avoiding the imposition of the missionary culture.

The Usefulness of Missio Dei

We have already indicated the usefulness of the *missio Dei* concept in providing a framework for placing God (in particular, the Trinity) at the centre of our thinking about mission.

The Trinitarian focus of *missio Dei,* combined with the focus on the Kingdom of God rescues the church from simply becoming an agent for social and economic change on the one hand or fundamentalism on the other[66] and provides a framework for mission in which the false dichotomy between social action and evangelism in mission can be eradicated. "The core of *missio Dei* is evangelism, the communication of the Gospel"[67] but this does not mean that we can turn our backs on the world and its needs. The call to conversion is a call to be witnesses to Christ by demonstrating his love and concern for the world.[68] An emphasis on *missio Dei* could be of great help to Evangelical churches in enabling them to overcome the sort of simplistic view of mission of which Chai complains, above.

Schrieter[69] suggests two possible domains in which *missio Dei* becomes a useful concept in a post-modern world.

> ... the unity in diversity of the Trinity will be a key for a theology of religious and cultural pluralism that is the mark of postmodern thought and civilization. Second, Trinitarian existence provides a strong theological foundation for mission as a dialogical process of giving and receiving ... speaking out prophetically and opening oneself for critique.

---

[66] Suess p.552
[67] Guder 2000 p. 49
[68] Guder 2000 p.120
[69] Quoted in Bevans and Schroeder p.293

The concepts of mission in a pluralistic society and prophetic dialogue are ones which Evangelicals need to explore in more depth. The traditional declamatory—confrontational, even—evangelical approach to mission is becoming increasingly less culturally appropriate as pluralism expands. There is a real need to discover ways in which the truths of Christianity can be explored in a society which rejects claims of absolute truth and which sees all religious opinions as being equally valid. Meditation on the nature of the Trinity could be useful in exploring these ideas.

Missio Dei, not only provides a theological key for mission in a post-modern age, it could also provide a motivational factor in a Western church which struggles internally with the challenges of post-modernism, pluralism and globalization. Interest in mission is declining among Evangelical churches in the West.[70] In part, this seems to be due to the impact of a post-modern mindset which sees all human narratives as being of equal value and importance. In this context, Christians become reluctant to "impose" their views on others. Equally, many Western churches offer a vast panoply of opportunities for Christian service with mission being simply "what some people do." *Missio Dei* elevates mission from the level of human activities, rightly showing mission as being participation in something which God is already doing. Evangelism is thus no longer elevating one human opinion over and above another equally valid one. There is a clear divine sanction for mission and evangelism (as well as a motivation for an culturally sensitive approach) which are no longer simply activities of the Church, but are, rather, the principal *raison d'être* of the Church.

Over the past two hundred years, Evangelical missionaries, motivated for the most part by the *Great Commission* (Matthew 28:16-20) have played a key role in spreading the Christian message around the world. The call to 'go and make disciples' was

---

[70] Dowsett p.449

necessary in an age when the geographical spread of Christianity was so limited. However, the great commission with its stress on activity plays into one of the weaknesses of Evangelicalism which so often stresses activity over and above spirituality. Gurder speaks reproachfully of people who are not actively experiencing the blessings of the Gospel, seeking to engage in mission.[71] There is a need for some evangelicals to step back from a focus on activity and the target driven approach of much of their missiology and to rediscover a theocentric view of mission which emphasizes character and spirituality over and above activity. *Missio Dei* and reflection on what many see as the key verse for Trinitarian mission, John 20:21 could provide the missing dimension.

The undeniable fact that *missio Dei* can still cover a wider range of meanings does place a potential limitation to its usefulness as a theological term. Equally, its association with secularized missiology means that some Evangelicals will be reluctant to use it to describe their own activities. However, there is no doubt that the underlying notions of theocentric, Trinitarian mission are ones which need to be explored further in Evangelical circles.

References

Bevans. S. B. & R. P. Schroeder.
> *Constants in Conflict: A Theology of Mission for Today.* Maryknoll.
> NY. Orbis Books. 2004

Bosch, D.J.
> *Transforming Mission: Paradigm Shifts in Theology of Mission.*
> New York: Orbis Books. 1991

Chai, Soo-Il.
> Missio Dei —Its development and Limitations in Korea.
> *International Review of Mission*, Vol. 92, Issue 367, 2003, p.
> 538-549.

---

[71] Guder 2000 p.151

Dowsett, R.
> Dry Bones in the West. In *Global Missiology for the 21st Century:
> Reflections from the Iguassu Dialogue*, ed. W. D. Taylor.
> (Grand Rapids: Baker Academic, 2001) pp. 447-462

Englesviken, T.
> Missio Dei: The Understanding and Misunderstanding of a
> Theological Concept in European Churches and Missiology.
> *International Review of Mission*, Vol. 92, Issue 367, 2003.

Goheen, M.
> *'As the Father has sent me, I am sending you': J.E. Lesslie Newbigin's
> missionary ecclesiology'* 2001 http://igitur-
> archive.library.uu.nl/dissertations/1947080/inhoud.htm

Guder, D. L. (ed.)
> *Missional Church: A Vision for the Sending of the Church in North
> America*. Cambridge. Eerdmans 1998

Guder, D. L.
> *The Continuing Conversion of the Church*. Cambridge: Eerdmans,
> 2000.

Hoffmeyer, John F.
> The Missional Trinity. *Dialog: A Journal of Theology*, Vol. 40
> Issue 2, June 2001, p. 108.

Kirk, J.A.
> *What is Mission? Theological Explorations*. (London, Darton,
> Longman and Todd, 1999)

Lee, D T-W.
> A Two Thirds World Evaluation of Contemporary Evangelical
> Missiology. In *Global Missiology for the 21st Century:
> Reflections from the Iguassu Dialogue*, ed. W. D. Taylor.
> (Grand Rapids: Baker Academic, 2001) pp. 133-148

Matthey, J.
> *Grezenlos—Boundless.* 50th anniversary of the World Mission
> Conference. Mission Festival and Congress. Missio Dei:
> God's Mission Today. (Reflectors Report). http://www.wcc-
> coe.org/wcc.what/mission/willingen.html

Newbigin, L.
   The Open Secret: An Introduction to the Theology of Mission.
   (London, SPCK 1995)

Philips, T. V.
   Edinburgh to Salvador: Twentieth Century Ecumenical Missiology.
   (Delhi India, ISPCK 1999) http://www.religion-
   online.org/showbook.asp?title=1573

Pachuau, L.
   Missiology in a Pluralistic World. *International Review of Mission*
   October 2000 http://www.religion-online.org

Recker, R. R.
   Concept of the Missio Dei and Instruction in Mission at Calvin
   Seminary. *Source: Calvin Theological Journal,* 11 N 1976

Richebacher, W.
   Missio Dei: the Basis of Mission Theology or a Wrong Path.
   International Review of Mission, Vol. 92 Issue 367, 2003, p.
   588-605.

Smith, W. C.
   Mission, Dialogue and God's Will for Us. *International Review of
   Mission,* No. 307, 1988, pp. 360-374.

Suess, P.
   Missio Dei and the Project of Jesus: The Poor and the "Other" as
   Mediators of the Kingdom of God and Protagonists of the
   Churches. *International Review of Mission*, Vol. 92 Issue 367,
   2003, p. 550-559.

Sundermeier, T.
   Missio Dei Today: on the Identity of Christian Mission.
   International Review of Mission, Vol. 92 Issue 367, 2003, p.
   560-578.

Taylor, W. D. ed.
   The Iguassu Affirmation. In *Global Missiology for the 21st Century:
   Reflections from the Iguassu Dialogue*, ed. W. D. Taylor.
   (Grand Rapids: Baker Academic, 2001) pp. 15-21

Wicker , P. L.

    Mission from the Margins: The Missio Dei in the Crisis of World Christianity. *International Review of Mission* no 369, 2004, pp. 182-199.

HOLISTIC HELP FOR THE PEOPLES OF THIS EARTH: FROM SUDAN TO SWITZERLAND

Kirk Franklin

Statement #1: The mission of Jesus was carried out through his words, deeds and signs and the people he focused on were often the poor and marginalized.

Identifying the Problems

This is a synthesis of the greatest problems of communities that face significant poverty and marginalization issues. The sources are five organizations and individuals who have analyzed what they believe to be the greatest challenges facing the world today. [1]

These 12 issues are faced by marginalized communities we serve. Therefore addressing these issues through various partnerships is part and parcel of serving them in a holistic sense (the proclamation and demonstration of the Gospel).

---

[1] [The sources are: a) United Nations University (research arm of the UN)—15 Global Challenges that humanity faces in the new millennium; b) J.F. Rischard, World Bank—twenty most pressing issues facing the global community; c) Rick Warren, pastor and author of *The Purpose Driven Life* developed the PEACE Plan to attack five global, evil giants of our day; d) Millennium Development Goals—a set of time bound and measurable goals and targets for combating major problems faced by developing nations; and e) The Copenhagen Consensus Center—an analysis of the world's greatest challenges cost efficient solutions to meeting these challenges; quoted in *Everything Must Change* by Brian McLaren.]

1. Proclamation of the gospel as the solution to spiritual hunger
2. Concerted effort to deal with climate change and ensure environmental sustainability
3. Sustainable clean drinking water
4. Eradication of extreme poverty and hunger
5. Sustainable development with increased economic opportunities
6. Provision of education in the fight against illiteracy
7. Control and treatment of malaria and global infectious diseases
8. Prevention of the spread of HIV/AIDs
9. Reduction of civil wars and ethnic tensions
10. Reduction of infant-child mortality
11. Improvement of the status of women
12. Addressing corrupt leadership and governance issues

In regards to seeking solutions to these crises it is worth noting Albert Einstein's statement: "No problem can be solved from the same level of consciousness that created it." Solutions for problems of this magnitude do not get found just by looking within the systems that created them. The solutions may lie elsewhere.

Finding Solutions

For Christians involved in the mission of God, with "mission" being "the committed participation of God's people in the purposes of God for the redemption of the whole of creation" (Chris Wright, The Mission of God), we have a responsibility to grapple with the solutions to these problems. The mission belongs to God but he "has a church for his mission in the world" (Wright). That 'mission... describes everything the church is sent into the world to do' (John Stott).

Therefore the approach Christians should make is to ask these questions:

1. What does God say in the Bible about these problems?
2. Why hasn't Christianity made a difference equal with its message, size, and resources?
3. What would need to happen for the church to make a positive difference?

The latest research suggests there are 77,000 people becoming Christians every day and 70,000 (or 91%) of these can be found in Africa, Asia, and Latin America. [*Missiometrics 2008: Reality Checks for Christian World Communions* prepared by David B. Barrett, a contributing editor, Todd M. Johnson, and Peter F. Crossing (www.WorldChristianDatabase.org)]

This rapid growth of the church of the Southern Continents presents a challenge when the global church considers what its response should be to the biggest problems facing the world's poor and marginalized peoples. This growth has these implications:

- Global plans of mission are increasingly initiated and led by Christians of the Global South.
- The perception of Christianity as a Western religion is disintegrating.

The Search for *Shalom*

To answer this question let us consider the Old Testament concept of *shalom*. In the Hebrew Old Testament the word is used 397 times. Its Greek equivalent *eirene* is used 89 times in the New Testament. Such heavy usage indicates the importance of this concept in both Hebrew and early Christian thought. *Shalom* means wholeness, without injury, wellbeing, a satisfactory condition, health, completeness, soundness, peace, well-being, prosperity and salvation. It is about the way the world ought to be. It implies a state of mind that is at peace and is satisfied, nothing is lacking, and social relationships are characterized by harmony and mutual support. It is a new community that breaks down the barriers of language, economy, race, gender and nationalism. It is a community transformed by the Gospel of Jesus Christ that is called to make peace, to seek social justice, provision of the needy including widows and orphans, and the poor and the protection of the exploited and the oppressed.

Shalom is based on three important principles:

- The earth and all that is in it belongs to God.
- Peoples of all nations share equally in God's loving concern because God is above favouritism and shows none to anyone—no person, people group, language or nation is above the other in God's eyes.
- The reign of God in creation leads to peace, justice and truly fulfilled lives.

Integral Mission

The Micah Network uses the term 'integral mission' which they define as holistic transformation or the proclamation and demonstration of the gospel. The vision is holistic as it touches on all areas of life. It is in planting and enabling of local churches to transform the communities of which they are part. The fruit is integral discipleship involving the responsible and sustainable use of the resources of God's creation and the transformation of the moral, intellectual, economic, cultural and political dimensions of our lives.

Any vision for a better human future that is Christian must include a vibrant, growing, living Christian community that is eagerly and joyfully serving God and the community. It is impossible to imagine a transforming community without a transforming church in its midst. Such a church is in love with God and with all its neighbors, celebrating everything that is for life and being a prophetic voice, telling the truth about everything that is against or that undermines life.

> Statement #2: As followers of Jesus, Wycliffe personnel focus on minority people groups so that they can hear God talk in their language.

How Can Wycliffe's Experience Be Made Fruitful for the Proclamation of the Gospel Here and Now?

When the Scriptures are placed into someone's hands in a poor rural area of Africa or Asia, how can a vision of *shalom* be given that provides hope in the midst of desperate conditions? The dignity and identity of all people and nations is related to God's plan of salvation. It is critical for those in the poverty trap to understand that they are made in God's image and therefore Christ came to earth to save them. The restoration of relationships is at the heart of total transformation. This includes the relationship with the triune God, relationships within people's community and the relationship with the environment.

The disciplines associated with Bible translation (literacy, sociolinguistics, ethnomusicology, anthropology, linguistics and translation, etc.) have a holistic focus because they have the end in mind of bringing about transformational change. Together they empower the marginalised and compel the powerful to recognise their weakness. Furthermore the spiritual understanding gained from the vernacular scriptures encourages spiritual maturity within the emerging Christian communities. They are also no longer dependent upon the outside world and are equipped to do theology in their context and apply this to daily life. This is the transformational change that Wycliffe longs to see take place around the world.

Case Study: Lamnso, Northwest Cameroon

Can a community of *shalom* be an outgrowth of a Bible translation project? In northwest Cameroon there are about 200,000 speakers of the Lamnso language. The Lamnso New Testament which was facilitated by Wycliffe Canadian linguists Karl and Winnie Grebe and published in 1990. Church leaders told me this New Testament "has been very much appreciated and it is being used." The desire to have the Old Testament came from the churches and they are supporting the project financially and have assigned the eight pastors and church workers who comprise the translation team. There is also a group of 20 reviewers and checkers. The church leaders stated the scriptures were essential to "effectively do worship, evangelism, discipleship and church planting in all areas."

Lamnso translators visit the churches to sensitize local church leaders and the Christians, encouraging mother tongue Scripture use and mother tongue literacy through the Church-Based Literacy Program using scripture booklets. At the Ministry of Agriculture and Rural Development Community Education and Action Center their Director said, "The Lamnso Bible translation project has done much for our center especially in the area of morally bringing up our youth and the perception of our mother tongue and the Lamnso language." At the center I visited a class of about 20 people learning about HIV-AIDS using materials developed by Wycliffe called "Kande's Story." The students gave speeches about what they had learned about the disease and how to avoid getting it and how to deal with its aftermath if it struck their families. As part of their course they were doing a formal Bible lessons led by a local pastor. The translation project was impacting the entire community.

The Bible Is Translatable

The Bible as God's living word speaks for itself in all situations because the Gospel is infinitely translatable and is intended for everyone regardless of what language they speak. There is no sacred culture or language that is the only medium that God can use. Jesus spoke Aramaic, a dialect of Hebrew. However the Gospels are already a translation from Hebrew or Aramaic into the Greek that was the vernacular of the early church. The message of Jesus is already a translation. Christianity abandoned the language and birthplace of its founder. This enabled it, often in a spontaneous way, moving from place to place to take on the languages of the peoples of the world "without the top-heavy infrastructure of institutions, so as to take root among simple people as well as in cities and towns."

Empires Impact Holistic Mission

The five centuries since 1500 have been marked by the rise of a series of empires, most of which have been European. These empires have not been stable and most ultimately have not lasted. That is not to say their influence has not lasted. For example, take the decisions made at the 1884-5 *Berlin Conference* where 14 colonial powers (such as Spain, Portugal, Italy, Great Britain, France, Germany and Belgium) met to carve up Africa. Dividing up the African continent was done with subjective divisions being made. Gaining new territory was the aim as all powers wanted to expand their empires and influence.

The first Kenyan president, Jomo Kenyatta said, "When the missionaries came to Africa they had the Bible and we had the land. They said, 'Let us pray.' We closed our eyes. When we opened them we had the Bible and they had the land." Archbishop Desmond Tutu (during the apartheid years when speaking to white Christian leaders) would say: "Now my brothers, based on this Bible you have given us, I call you to give us back our land!"

By 1945 all of these empires had fallen or were on the verge of collapse. The US emerged from WWII as the leading world power, although the USSR soon was a strong rival and was seen as a threat until its collapse in 1990. But empires are never permanent and are very sensitive to whatever threatens their dominance. Even as many are speaking of the decline of American empire, other experts are discussing the emerging empires of China and India.

Nations engaged in colonialism would find it hard to face the full dimensions of Jesus' essential message since it would, if they saw it, call into question the whole colonial project.

	Colonial	Post-colonial
Colonizers	Felt powerful, clean, knowledgeable, superior, capable, civilized	Looking back now feel ashamed, humbled, repentant, uncertain, conciliatory regretful
Colonized	Felt dirty, ashamed, grateful, dependent, incompetent, incapable, uneducated, unintelligent, resentful, abused, afraid	Now because it is in the distant past, feel competent, capable, hopeful, confident, empowered
The Gospel	The Gospel of avoiding hell	The Gospel of the Kingdom of God [Ref. Brian McLaren]

Conclusion

"God created the world as good, but human beings—as individuals and as groups—have rebelled against God and filled the world with evil and injustice" (Brian McLaren). However God's plan for the world is that all persons everywhere, in every nation, know God's salvation and be delivered from disobedience, disruption, despair, disease and all that destroys our wholeness.

Wycliffe seeks to be a catalyst for God's solutions for the poor and marginalized communities of the world. And it seeks to encourage the church and other organizations to become active in this concern for these communities.

SHALOM:
THE GOAL OF THE KINGDOM AND
OF INTERNATIONAL DEVELOPMENT

Beth Snodderly

> The Kingdom of God is ... righteousness, peace, and joy
> (Romans 14:17).

The Need for Shalom

> They made my brother hold a flashlight and watch while they
> took turns raping me. They were like animals. When he refused
> their order to rape me, they stabbed him to death in front of my
> eyes, just as they had done with my parents a year ago.

For eight months this Congolese woman was a slave to the Congolese rebel army, raped multiple times every day, until she finally managed to escape. Reunited with her children, whom she had thought dead, she is now raising her new baby, Hope, the child of one of her rapists, while she participates in a job training program designed for women like herself. This woman's plight is common in the Congo, where in some rural villages 90% of the women have been raped, ages 3 to 73. The only doctor in the only hospital on the "front lines" of this civil war, who does his best to repair torn and broken bodies, is the only man the women who come to him have been able to trust. Their husbands often leave them, this doctor recognizes, because they have been humiliated by being powerless to defend their women.

In a resource-rich country, this systematic destabilization of the society through violent acts against the women, enables certain interest groups to rape the natural resources of the land for their own benefit.

(Summary of "War against Women: The Use of Rape as a Weapon in Congo's Civil War," a "60 Minutes" segment, televised January 13, 2008, CBS News.)

Compare the condition of this society to that described by the prophet Isaiah in 59:4-11: No one calls for justice; no one pleads his case with integrity. ... They conceive trouble and give birth to evil. ... Their deeds are evil deeds, and acts of violence are in their hands. Their feet rush into sin; they are swift to shed innocent blood. Their thoughts are evil thoughts; ruin and destruction mark their ways. The way of peace they do not know; there is no justice in their paths. They have turned them into crooked roads; no one who walks in them will know peace. So justice is far from us, and righteousness does not reach us. We look for light, but all is darkness; for brightness, but we walk in deep shadows. Like the blind we grope along the wall, feeling our way like men without eyes. At midday we stumble as if it were twilight; among the strong, we are like the dead. ... We look for justice, but find none; for deliverance, but it is far away.

Questions

1. What is wrong with these two societies? How do societies get to the place where such unrestrained violence and corruption break out?

2. What does God want human life to look like?

3. What are the essential conditions for a society to experience wholeness, peace and safety?

4. What is the responsibility of the body of Christ to those in harm's way? What should be the role of Kingdom-minded international development workers in addressing the roots of human problems around the world and what opposition should they expect to face?

Shalom Word Study

Before setting out to "solve" the problems of the world it is important to know the goal toward which one is working. What does God want human life to look like? One way to approach answers to that question, and the others above, is to survey the connotations of the Hebrew word *shalom*, commonly translated "peace," but which implies much more: wholeness and wellness in the context of right relationships with God, people, and nature. This article intends to engage in an ongoing dialog about the relationship between advancing God's Kingdom and doing "international development," through a survey of the context of the occurrences of the word, "*shalom*," in the Old Testament, with some comparisons to the New Testament. The usage and context of several Greek words for "*shalom*" that were used by the translators of the Septuagint, will be the basis for this study. (See a comprehensive list at the end of this article, "*Shalom*: Right Relationships with God, People, and Nature.") The descriptions of *shalom* will be seen to correspond with descriptions of God's will for people and all creation. But there is an enemy actively opposing God's will. The theme of the Bible is the battle for the rulership of this world. In John 12:31 Jesus says of his upcoming death, "now the ruler of this world is being driven out." A summary in 1 John 3:8 of the purpose of Jesus' appearing on earth says, "the Son of God came to destroy the works of the devil." Those who participate with the Son of God in this battle will face the conditions the enemy seeks to impose: "the whole world lies in the power of the evil one" (1 John 5:19). The plight of those lying in the evil one's power are described in the Old Testament, although the enemy's presence was not well recognized, in passages where the opposite of *shalom* is described.

Descriptions of the Absence of Shalom

Question 1. What is wrong with these two societies? How do societies get to the place where such unrestrained violence and corruption break out?

Many of the occurrences of the term *shalom,* in the Old Testament are in the context of conditions in which peace, safety and well-being are absent. These passages describe the opposite of God's will and illustrate principles for understanding what has gone wrong in societies experiencing violence and danger.

God judges evil societies

Old Testament history shows that God turns his back on those who do evil. He allows evil societies to be overthrown and destroyed, whether by the violence of other evil societies or natural disasters, or both (see Jeremiah 33:4-6 and 4:22-26). Ralph Winter has commented that it shows God's commitment to free will that innocent people and even believers suffer while God is allowing evil cultures and societies to burn themselves out and destroy one another. [1] Jeremiah pointed out to the people of Jerusalem, regarding the disasters and lack of *shalom* he prophesied were coming to them, "Your own conduct and actions have brought this upon you. This is your punishment" (4:18).

God deals with societies according to their own standards

In a land full of violence, God said he would deal with the people according to their conduct and judge them by their own standards (see Ezekiel 7:23-27). In seeking to understand the judgment of God against a society, questions such as these might be helpful:

What signs can be found in the history of the society of God's activity or redemptive analogies?

In what ways have the people, particularly the leaders, disobeyed and rebelled against what was right according to their own culture's traditional values?

What are the society's own expectations of justice and judgment?

---

[1] Comment in a private conversation with the author on February 14, 2008.

Nature is cursed when a society turns away from God

A person or group that presumes to think they are "safe and blameless" (Hebrew: *shalom*/ Greek: *hosia*) when in reality they are persisting in going their own way, contrary to God's way, will bring disaster on the land. "All the curses written in this book," listed in Deuteronomy 28:15ff, will come against that person or society, Moses warned (see Deut. 29:18, 19). Among the curses for those not following God's commands are "wasting disease, with fever and inflammation, with scorching heat and drought, with blight and mildew, which will plague you until you perish" (Deut. 28:22).

Descriptions of the Presence of Shalom

Question 2. What does God want human life to look like?

In contrast to the descriptions of the absence of *shalom*, descriptions of the presence of *shalom* illustrate God's will for people and the land. In a presentation to the staff of the U.S. Center for World Mission on February 14, 2008, Paul Pierson asked the question, "What does God want human life to look like?" He answered with a good description of *shalom*, which is also a good description of the goals of international development: grace, health, education, safety, well-being for all people.

These qualities flow from being in right relationship with God, as seen in Jeremiah's prophecy that tied the concept of "prosperity" (Hebrew: *shalom*/ Greek: *eirene*) to God's forgiveness of sins of rebellion. "I will ... forgive all their sins of rebellion against me. Then this city will bring me renown, joy, praise and honor before all nations on earth that hear of all the good things I do for it; and they will be in awe and will tremble at the abundant <u>prosperity and peace</u> I provide for it" (33:8, 9).

From this passage, it is clear that *shalom* is a quality that is observable. A visible evidence of *shalom* in the realm of nature was understood by one of Job's comforters as including the wild animals being at peace (Hebrew:*shalom*/ Greek *eirene)* with humans (Job 5:24). Isaiah elaborated on this concept in describing the reign of the

Messiah: "The wolf will live with the lamb, the leopard will lie down with the goat, the calf and the lion and the yearling together; and a little child will lead them. ... They will neither harm nor destroy on all my holy mountain, for the earth will be full of the knowledge of the Lord as the waters cover the sea" (11:6, 9).

In his list of animal life that will no longer harm or destroy when the Lord's *shalom* is being experienced, Isaiah's lack of knowledge prevented him from including harmful micro-organisms that cause disease in humans, animals, and plants. But knowing in the 21st century that disease is caused by bacteria and viruses, and knowing that disease is one of the curses that is an evidence of the lack of *shalom* (see Deut. 28:22 and Jer. 32:23), it seems reasonable to include the "taming" (or eradication) of these types of "animal" life in a contemporary application of the understanding of *shalom*.

Another observable sign of *shalom* is health and healing for a formerly wicked city and the people in it: "I will bring health and healing to [the city]; I will heal my people and will let them enjoy abundant peace/*eirene* and security (Greek *pistin*—the root word for faithfulness)" (Jer. 33:6). This passage demonstrates that there is no dichotomy between social and spiritual healing or between physical and spiritual healing. *Shalom* is holistic.

Conditions for Experiencing Shalom
Question 3. What are the essential conditions for a society to experience the wholeness, peace and safety described immediately above?

When a society repents and turns to God, Scripture shows, He is willing to restore and bless the people with *shalom/eirene* (see Ps. 30:11; Jer. 33: 6, 9). A concordance study shows there seem to be two conditions for a society or person to experience *shalom*. One is the intention to follow God's laws and principles. The other is acceptance of God's provision of a substitute punishment for *not* following God's laws and principles. In both cases opposition should be expected from the enemy whose goal is the opposite of God's will.

The principle of keeping God's requirements as a condition for blessing and *shalom* was specifically stated to Isaac shortly before he encountered Abimelech, king of the Philistines (see Genesis 26:1-5). It is through following God's guidelines that a society can function well. In fact, all nations on earth willing to function according to the will of God as revealed through His chosen people, will end up being blessed materially and spiritually (*shalom*). This is seen in Genesis 26:4, 5 where God repeated the promise to Isaac that was originally given to Abraham: "through your offspring all nations on earth will be blessed, because Abraham obeyed me and kept my requirements, my commands, my decrees and my laws." Immediately following this promise is an illustration of one of the nations, the Philistines, being blessed by the presence of Isaac's family, in spite of various problems, and sending him away in peace/*shalom*/*eirene* (Gen. 26:29, 30), without further quarreling or fighting.

When God's principles are followed, peace results. This is also seen in the encounter between Moses and his father-in-law. Jethro showed Moses how to satisfy the peoples' need for justice, without wearing himself, out by delegating some of the work to others. Jethro specifically stated that if "God so commands" that the principles of delegation be followed, and if Moses did follow them, then Moses would be able to stand the strain of leadership and the people would go home satisfied (*shalom*/"in peace"). (See Exodus 18:7-23.)

But *shalom* does not come easily. A spiritual enemy has it as his goal to prevent *shalom*; to prevent God's will from being done. Broken relationships among people and with God characterize the activities of people and nations throughout the Old Testament. A pattern seen throughout the Major and Minor Prophets is the repeated description of God allowing one nation to punish another for their evil ways, with the focus on the people of Israel and Judah who had the most opportunity to know God's expectations, yet failed to follow Him. As God would withdraw His presence and hand of protection, the evil one, the "ruler of this world" (John 12:31) would step in and create havoc. The Old Testament prophets, without specifically acknowledging this enemy, recognized that God was somehow using or allowing one evil nation to punish another. Then the instrument of punishment of one group of people would in turn experience punishment for their own evil ways, in a seemingly never-ending cycle. (See, for example, Hosea 8:3-8; Joel 3:1-7.)

But a climactic statement by the prophet Isaiah points toward the possibility of a break in this vicious cycle. Speaking of the coming Messiah, Isaiah prophesied: "He was pierced for our transgressions, he was crushed for our iniquities; the punishment that brought us <u>peace</u> (*shalom/eirene*) was upon him, and by his wounds we are healed" (Is. 53:5). Jesus brought an end to the cycle of one society punishing another for the evils it commits in its rebellion against God. Jesus took the final punishment on behalf of any person or society that will accept his peace offering. This was the defeat of the evil one's schemes against humanity (1 John 3:8). By accepting this substitute punishment, people and societies can break out of the vicious cycle and experience healing of broken relationships with God, people, and nature.

The Battle for Shalom

Question 4. What is the responsibility of the body of Christ to those in harm's way? What should be the role of Kingdom-minded international development workers in addressing the roots of human problems around the world?

Jeremiah seemed to be saying, in his plea to Israel, that if God's people will obey him, the rest of the world will be blessed: "If you put your detestable idols out of my sight and no longer go astray, and if in a truthful, just and righteous way you swear, 'As surely as the Lord lives,' then the nations will be blessed by him and in him they will glory" (4:1,2). The challenge to be God's obedient people, who are experiencing some of that blessing, becomes very personal if we dare to ask ourselves the question from the Lord through the prophet Haggai: What are we doing building our paneled houses and elaborate landscapes when God's "Temple," the intended Body of Christ, is in shambles around the world? (see Haggai 1:3); when there are people from many nations in harm's way whom God wants to redeem for his glory (Is. 11:9)? What is the part of 21st-century believers in the battle for the planet?

Quoting again from Paul Pierson's presentation on February 14, 2008, "we are called to call people to become followers of Jesus as authentic disciples of Jesus in their culture and to show something to the world of what the Kingdom of God means, and what are its values." Pierson added, "What passion has God given you? If he gives you a passion He'll give you the gifts to go with it."

The Body of Christ contains people with the gifts to "do" or "make" *shalom* in many different areas: justice, peace-keeping, skill-building for economic independence, health, fighting and eradicating disease, etc. All of these peace-making activities can potentially demonstrate the values of the Kingdom and bring *shalom* into the lives of troubled people and societies. Jesus concluded his farewell speech to his disciples by promising *shalom* in the midst of trouble: "I have told you these things, so that in me you may have peace/*eirene*. In this world you will have trouble. But take heart! I have overcome the world" (John 16:33). In 1 John we see that believers in Jesus also overcome the world and the evil one who rules it (1 John 2:13, 14; 5:4). As a result they are able to enjoy and pass on to others the *shalom* of God, as seen in the greetings of 2 John and 3 John. Compare the Greek words in these greetings with the list of words found at the end of this article showing how the Septuagint translated *shalom*:

"Grace/*charis*, mercy/*eleos* and peace/*eirene* from God the Father and from Jesus Christ, the Father's Son, will be with us in truth and love" (2 John 3).

"Dear friend, I pray that you may enjoy good health/*hugiainei* and that all may go well with you, even as your soul is getting along well" (3 John 2).

Concluding Challenge

What will it take for a society that is not enjoying "good health," that is engulfed in evil and experiencing the absence of God's presence, to get to the place where it experiences *shalom*? What would *shalom* look like in the Congo, in Sudan, in Iraq, in Myanmar? Contrast the unjust and violent conditions in such societies with Zechariah's prophesy, as he sings and prophesies to his baby son, John the Baptist, in Luke 1:68-79:

> Praise be to the Lord, the God of Israel, because he has come and has redeemed his people.
>
> He has raised up a horn of salvation for us in the house of his servant David (as he said through his holy prophets of long ago),
>
> salvation from our enemies and from the hand of all who hate us—to show mercy to our fathers and to remember his holy covenant, the oath he swore to our father Abraham:
>
> to rescue us from the hand of our enemies, and to enable us to serve him without fear in holiness and righteousness before him all our days.
>
> And you, my child, will be called a prophet of the Most high: for you will go on before the Lord to prepare the way for him,
>
> to give his people the knowledge of salvation through the forgiveness of their sins, because of the tender mercy of our God,
>
> to shine on those living in darkness and in the shadow of death, to guide our feet into the path of peace/*eirene*.

Zechariah sang about salvation from human enemies, about serving God without fear in holiness and righteousness, forgiveness, mercy, peace—the same *shalom* spoken of throughout the Old Testament. In the context of similar justice, righteousness and faithfulness, Isaiah described "salvation" from feared enemies in the realm of nature (which can also represent disease micro-organisms that were unknown at that time): "The wolf will live with the lamb, the leopard will lie down with the goat, ... and a little child will lead them. They will neither harm nor destroy on all my holy mountain, for the earth will be full of the knowledge of the Lord" (Is. 11:6, 9).

In the wholistic nature of *shalom,* there is no dichotomy between physical and spiritual health and well-being. *Shalom* is the description of God's will for the earth and everything living in it. *Shalom* is the goal of international development because this is the goal of the Kingdom: "Our Father in heaven ... your kingdom come, your will be done on earth as it is in heaven" (Matthew 6:10). Believers need to ready for serious opposition in the spiritual battle for the rulership of this world. Jesus came and "made peace" by his death on the cross. Believers should expect no less opposition than he faced when they join him as "sons of God" in making (waging) peace in a broken war-torn world.

> "Blessed are the peacemakers for they will be called sons of God" (Matthew 5:9).

Shalom: Wholeness and Right Relationships with God, People, and Nature

Occurrences and Meanings in the Septuagint of the Greek Words Used to Translate the Hebrew *Shalom*

hugiainei 10x
Wellness, physical health   Gen. 29:6; 37:14; 43:27,28; 2 Sam. 20:9; Esther 9:30; Is. 9:6
Greeting (I wish you well, peace to you, good health to you, prosperity to you) Ex. 4:18; 1 Sam. 25:6
Farewell (go in peace/health)   2 Sam. 15:9

sotarias 3x
Safety ("salvation") Gen. 26:31; 41:16; 44:17

hileos 1x
God deal mercifully with you, fear not Gen. 43:23

hosia 1x
Let good happen to me Deut. 29:19

anepause 1x
God has given me rest round about (no one is plotting against me) 1 Kings 4:24

euthenousi 1x
Their houses are safe (good condition; no rod of punishment from God is upon them) Job 21:9

chairein 3x
No joy to the wicked Is. 48:22; 57:21
Go out with joy, and be led forth with peace/gladness Is. 55:12

teleian 1x
Wholly carried away (Hebrew: peacefully exiled) Jer. 13:19

eirenes 169x
Die peacefully Gen. 15:15; 2 Kings 22:20; 2 Chron. 34:28; Jer. 34:5
Speak peaceably, kindly, absence of deceit   Gen. 37:4; Deut. 20:10; Ps. 28:3; 35:20; 120:7; Prov. 12:20; Is. 52:7; Jer. 9:8; Nah. 1:15; Zech. 9:10

Satisfied that justice has been done Ex. 18:23

Absence of quarrelling, war, fighting, or danger Gen 26:29; Lev. 26:6; Deut. 2:26; 20:11; 23:61; Josh. 9:15; Jud 4:17; 8:9; 11:13; 21:13; 1 Sam 7:14; 16:4, 5; 2 Sam. 15:27; 19:24, 30; 1 Kings 2:5,13; 5:12; 22:27,28; 2 Kings 9:17,18,19,22,31; 1 Chron. 12:17; 2 Chron. 15:5; Ps. 120:6; 122:6,7,8; 147:14; Eccl 3:8; Is. 27:5; 33:7; 57:2; Jer. 4:10; 6:14; 8:11,15; 12:5; 23:17; 28:9; Eze. 7:25; Mic. 3:5; Zech. 6:13; 8:10

God's favor/covenant; associated with truth, doing good, righteousness, obedience, healing Num 6:26; 25:12; 1 Kings 2:33; 2 Kings 20:19; 1 Chron. 22:9; Ps. 30:11; 34:14; 37:11,37; 72:3,7; 85:8,10; 119:165; 125:5; 128:6; Prov. 3:2; Song of Sol 8:10; Is. 26:3; 26:12; 32:17; 39:8; 45:7; 48:18; 53:5; 54:13; 57:19; 59:8; 60:17; Jer. 12:12; 14:13,19; 16:5; 29:11; 33:6; Lam 3:17; Eze. 34:25; 37:26; Mic. 5:5; Hag 2:9; Zech. 8:16,19; Mal. 2:5

Safe, secure Josh. 10:21; 1 Sam. 20:7,13,21; 2 Sam. 3:21,22, 23; 17:3; 18:29,32 1 Kings 22:17; 2 Chron. 18:16; 2 Chron. 18:27; Ezra 9:12; Job 5:24; Ps. 4:8 Prov. 3:17; Is. 32:18; 41:3; Jer. 25:37; 30:5; 43:12; Eze. 13:10,16

Greeting (peace be to thee; how are you) Jud. 6:23; 18:15; 19:20; 1 Sam 10:4; 25:5; 30:21; 2 Sam. 8:10; 11:7; 2 Kings 10:13; 1 Chron. 12:18; Dan. 10:19

Farewell [go in peace] Jud 18:6; 1 Sam. 1:17; 20:42; 29:7; 2 Sam. 11:7; 2 Kings 5:19

All is well/ is it well? 2 Sam. 18:28; 2 Kings 4:23,26; 5:21; 9:11; Jer. 15:5

Prosperity Job 15:21; Ps. 35:27; 73:3; Is. 66:12; Jer. 29:7; 33:9; 38:4

Friend [man of peace] Ps. 41:9; Jer. 38:22; Obadiah 7

ECONOMIC JUSTICE FOR THE POOR

David Befus and Stephen Bauman

And what does the LORD require of you? To do justice, love
mercy, and walk humbly with your God (Micah 6:8).

A theologian was preaching on the nature of injustice
when a group of Latin American women called out, "We
know what justice is—it is bread for our children."[1] In a
world where more than a billion people live on less than
one dollar a day, business moguls earn more than the economic
output of entire nations and malnourished countries export their
grain to the highest bidder, the notion of *economic justice* has
never been more relevant. Living as Christians today, surely we
must ask, "What does the Lord require of us?"

The Biblical Foundation of Economic Justice

We serve a God who loves justice (Isaiah 61:8; Psalm 11:7; 33:5;
37:28; 99:4), delights in it (Jeremiah 9:23), demands it (Deuteronomy
16:20) and executes it for the needy (Psalm 140:13). He leads with it
(Isaiah 9:7), promises it (Isaiah 42:3) and ultimately judges us with it
(Isaiah 58:6). He is the "God of justice" (Isaiah 30:18) and requires us
to "do justice" (Micah 6:8) as a community of faith. While the Bible
does not present a systematic treatise on economic justice, it offers a
profound paradigm on economic justice through the hundreds of
texts scattered throughout the Old and New Testaments. While not
comprehensive, the following statements attempt to summarize the
biblical vision of economic justice:

---

[1] Duncan Forrester, *Christian Justice and Public Policy* (Cambridge: Cambridge
University Press), 55.

(a) Economic justice originates in God's nature and character. Justice is a moral attribute of God and is indispensable to his nature and moral character (Isaiah 30:18). Because economic justice is one dimension of justice it is, therefore, rooted in God's nature and character. Given the fact that God's Trinitarian nature is relational, justice (economic and otherwise) is not an abstract, but relational concept.

(b) The biblical vision for justice is founded in God's creative act in history. Every person is created in the image of God (Genesis 1) and endowed with great creative potential (value, conscience, gifts, talents, and creativity). God's creation is a gift to all, not to be appropriated for the benefit of only a few and to deny dignity or opportunity to any one person desecrates the image of God.

(c) God worked for six days in designing the world, and He created man in His image to work productively. The Christian notion of work implies *calling,* as expressed by the German reformation word *beruf,* meaning "a task set by God." The encouragement to work is founded (Genesis 2:15) and presented throughout the Scriptures and the expectation that those who follow God's path for their lives will *"work with your hands... so that your life may win the respect of outsiders and so that you will not be dependent on anybody"* (1 Thessalonians 4:11). Jesus teaches us to pray *"give us this day our daily bread,"* (Matthew 6) and work, not alms, is the foundation for the realization of that prayer.

(d) Sin has corrupted God's plan for economic justice. The idea that economic activity "benefits consumers and maximizes efficient utilization of the earth's scarce resources"[2] has proven false due to man's sinful nature evident in greed, corruption and the concentration of resources in the hands of a few. Evil is

---

[2] Robert Gilpin, *Global Political Economy* (Princeton, NJ: Princeton University Press, 2001), 23.

manifested not only in the behavior of individuals, but also in structural evils that preserve the wealth of upper classes. However, the *love* of money, not money in and of itself, is evil. In spite of the fall, the field of economics is legitimate and, in fact, based in God's cultural mandate (Genesis 1:26-28). Put simply, wealth is a resource, and economics a tool.

(e) Economic justice demands righteous relationships. Economic justice is not only concerned with a sense of what is right, or what *should* happen, but with a righteous heart in relationship to God (vertical) and within society (horizontal). The relationship of the members of the divine Trinity provides the theological paradigm for our social mandate to serve in and through community.

(f) The biblical vision of economic justice is redemptive. The reconciliation of "all things" in Christ (Colossians 1:20) includes the economic realm. The scriptures link justice with deliverance from oppression (Judges 5:11), freedom from captivity (Isaiah 41:1-11) and salvation (Psalm 79:6; Isaiah 63:1). The biblical foundation of human dignity, coupled with the emphasis on love for our neighbour (Genesis 4:9, Luke 10:33), implies that we must seek reconciliation in *all* areas of life, including the economic sphere.

(g) We are called to steward wealth in a manner that extends the Kingdom of God. "The earth is the Lord's and everything in it" (Psalm 24:1). He is the only absolute owner (Leviticus 25:23); we are merely commissioned as stewards (Genesis 1:29-30). When God blesses and gives wealth (Deuteronomy 8:18), it is for the purpose of making his ways known on the earth and his salvation among all nations (Psalm 67:2). While God can and does, allow the accumulation of wealth through unjust means he does not condone it. God takes into account how and on what basis, wealth has been accumulated and stewarded (Isaiah 58). As Christians, we enjoy the profound privilege of participating with God in the

administration of His kingdom, which includes the creation of economies that respect and nurture the dignity and worth of every human being.

Finally, while the biblical vision of justice allows for economic differences, it condemns significant disparity in society as unjust and holds us accountable for economic injustice (Isaiah 58). While *equality of income* is not necessarily the biblical norm for equity, *equality of opportunity* is perfectly in line with biblical principles. In short, economic differences are "morally acceptable, even, in fact, morally necessary,"[3] but only to a certain extent.

(h) The biblical vision of economic justice is restorative. The scriptures present a restored, just economy that contains a "dynamic, community-building character" (Isaiah 63:1). We recognize that restoration, *shalom*, is not possible without justice. Human life unfolds between the first and second creations (Romans 8:18-25) and it is here where God requires us to demonstrate justice measured by our treatment of the powerless in society (Isaiah 58:6). We also recognize the biblical mandate calls us to care for the environment (Genesis 2:15). Finally, this vision of restored creation (Isaiah 11:4-6; 25:1-8), where love and justice govern (Psalm 9:7-8), begins here and now. However, in keeping with the already/not yet view of the Kingdom of God, we must seek to effect change in this life while recognizing that perfect economic justice will only be achieved with the final coming of the Kingdom.

The Church's Mandate

The church has a biblical mandate to embrace, pursue, and model economic justice.

Indeed, economic justice is integral to holistic mission and it is incumbent upon the church to take a leading role in addressing issues of economics and injustice, both at the macro and micro levels. It should be mentioned, however, that confronting this

---

[3] Ron Sider, *Just Generosity* (Grand Rapids, MI: Baker Books, 1999), 67.

problem is complex, and, thus, we should not expect clear-cut solutions for the world economy. Often, instead, in evaluating economic issues, we encounter trade-offs. Moreover, while "economic analysis allows us to measure reasonably well who the winners and losers from trade will be, and what they will win[19] or lose...[it] gives us no insights to judge which trade-offs are indeed most 'fair.'"[4] It is the church that must provide a clarion voice to the issues of economic justice.

A summary of the church's mandate is as follows:

(a) The church must pursue a holistic theology where economic justice is integral to its mission. It is morally incumbent upon the church to *embrace, model* and *teach* economic justice as an expression of the Kingdom of God.

(b) The church must embrace and teach a biblical understanding of the poor and poverty. It is essential to distinguish between various expressions of poverty, such as *poverty as oppression*, where compounding factors, often systemic and structural, leave the poor in a state of utter powerlessness;[5] *poverty of being*[6] where a "lifetime of suffering, deception, and exclusion is internalized by the poor in a way that results in the poor no longer knowing who they truly are or why they were created,[7] and; *poverty of spirit* (Matthew 5:3), which is, in essence, humility, or brokenness of heart—clearly a kingdom value sought and celebrated by Christians worldwide. How we understand poverty influences how we relate to the poor. Most importantly, we must be careful in labelling any

---

[4] Diane Whitmore, "Faithfulness and the Dismal Science," *Faith and International Affairs* (2003), 54.

[5] Christopher Heuertz, *The Cry* 8:3 (2002), 5.

[6] We must promote awareness, understanding, and engagement in the *local church*, on issues of economic justice, business as mission, and wealth and innovation. Specifically, we must encourage grassroots discussion and action groups at the local church level to deal with issues of economic injustice.

[7] Bryant Myers, *Walking with the Poor* (Maryknoll, NY: Orbis Books, 1999), 76.

person in view of the creative potential[8] with which God has endowed all of us, both individually (for example, value, innovation, conscience, talents, and gifts) and as a community (for example, the unique gifts of hospitality or perseverance in certain cultures).

(c) The church must demonstrate economic justice through word, deed and sign incarnationally, among the poor, involving the presence of the poor in the process of transformation. For economic justice to authentically occur, the poor must be actors in their own transformation, not merely receptors.

(d) The church has an indisputable mandate to care for the poor. There are more poor people today than ever before in history and in many cases they are getting poorer.[9] Jesus came to "lift up the humble, and to fill the hungry with good things" (Luke 1:53). As we follow this example, we must give special consideration to the impact of globalization on the poor. The ability of the poor to access capital, markets, and work are three critical factors that must be weighed in considering the effects of globalization.[10]

(f) The church has a prophetic mandate to denounce systemic and structural sins of injustice in business, government and culture, both at the national and international levels. Specifically, the church should be at the forefront of confronting the problem of an economic segment described by secular experts as "the bottom of the pyramid, where four billion people reside whose per capita income is less than $1,500 per

---

[8] Realized or unrealized creative potential, that is.

[9] Special consideration must be given to Sub-Saharan Africa, which accounts for only 1% of total world trade, is left out of the world economy, and continues to fall further behind.

[10] Capital tends to concentrate in the pockets of the upper classes, as does critical information about technology, prices, and transport requirements for imports or exports.

year."[11] As the church, we must take an active role in the public sphere where, for example, corruption is often present, but we must avoid the promotion of specific economic frameworks, whether capitalism, socialism, or other as it can result in the misuse of the Christian faith to legitimize practices that may not be compatible with the Christian worldview. Likewise, scrutiny and open-minded debate is required of macroeconomic policy.[12] Christians are often not aware of the economic impact of their country policy on the poor and needy populations of the world.

(g) At the same time, the church must prophetically announce economic justice within and without the church locally and globally through word, deed and sign. It is morally incumbent upon the church to grapple with, and seek to understand, the complex issues of economic justice. Out of this understanding, the church must teach and model economic justice as an expression of the Kingdom of God. As we seek to address issues of economic injustice, we must give consideration to the issues of freedom and equality. The promotion of *freedom* highlights individual rights and the free market for maximizing economic production. The promotion of *equality* focuses on how wealth is shared, and how profits are distributed. There is a difference between poverty and inequality; these are two separate issues. There are real world cases where inequality is high, but poverty is low and vice versa. There are also tradeoffs between poverty and inequality currently evident in globalization. God is concerned about both. Furthermore, as economic policy is considered, we need to differentiate the concept of absolute and relative comparisons of income and poverty.

---

[11] C. K. Prahalad, *The Future of Competition: Co-Creating Unique Value with Customers* (Cambridge, MA: Harvard Business School Press, 2004), 3.

[12] For example, U.S. representatives at the Doha round of GATT/WTO trade negotiations rightly criticized the European Union Common Agricultural Policy that provides huge export subsidies and impossible restrictions on agricultural imports, but then did not acknowledge the injustice of the steel tariffs, U.S. farm bill, and blockage of a deal that would have given poor countries access to cheap essential medicines (*Fortune*, 9/1/2003), 35.

(h) The church must prioritize its efforts in understanding and addressing economic injustice as both a cause and symptom of the global HIV/AIDS pandemic. In 2004, 8,000 people died each day from the HIV/AIDS pandemic, and the number continues to escalate. The church must respond holistically, recognizing that poverty is central to the HIV/AIDS issue.

(i) The church has a prophetic mandate to address lifestyle issues related to consumerism. Unfortunately, self-indulgent economic activity and materialism is promoted in some Christian communities as having intrinsic value, with no regard to Christian witness, responsibility to the poor, or any other objective except the affluent lifestyle of the "successful Christian." The market place is a context for ministry, but ministry only takes place if the people of God proclaim His word, show love and compassion, exercise stewardship of creation, and engage in spiritual warfare. Accumulating wealth for one's own material status is not inherently Christian, and is criticized by Jesus.

(j) The church must give a high priority towards searching out the causes of economic injustice as it relates to terrorism. September 11th, 2001 and events thereafter, underscore the importance of addressing the causes of terrorism, especially in understanding its relationship to economic injustice.

Action Steps

On Karl Marx's tomb in Highgate cemetery are inscribed the words "Philosophers have only interpreted the world. The point is, however, to change it." If we consider all that is written on the topic of economic justice, the same statement can be made. As we look to the future, we need more practical and constructive steps to promote change. However, we must remember the issues are complex. We need to avoid simplistic conclusions, and instead provide practical solutions rooted in biblical theology.

First and foremost, it is essential we engage the poor in the process of seeking economic transformation. As the non-poor, we must not merely integrate the poor into the discussion but, rather, through authentic relationship, recognize and embrace their voice *alongside and among* our own. This process must begin at the grassroots level, in churches, community groups and networks and trickle up to local, national, and international dialogue. We must begin by learning from the poor, in particular, their enormous capacity to daily survive economic injustice within their communities. Together, the non-poor and resource poor, *as one church*, must address issues of economic justice.

We, the Church of Jesus Christ, must speak and act prophetically on issues of economic injustice in the following ways:

1. We must promote awareness, understanding and engagement in the *local church*, on issues of economic justice, business as mission, wealth and innovation. Specifically, we must encourage grassroots discussion and action groups at the local church level to deal with issues of economic injustice.

2. We must urgently respond holistically to the HIV/AIDS pandemic, recognizing that poverty and economic injustice is central to the pandemic.

3. We must evaluate and change our patterns of consumption and promote a simple lifestyle to avoid contributing to global economic injustice.

4. We need to invest in women and children with the message of economic justice as a means of transforming the next generation.

5. We must promote biblical holistic worldview education in the church.

6. We must endorse, promote and implement holistic models of microfinance[13] and enterprise as solutions to economic injustice,

---

[13] The microfinance movement has been a significant means towards creating economic justice for the poor. Today thousands of microfinance institutions,

and consider the worldwide Christian business community as a resource to generate employment and increase incomes.

7. We must endorse and encourage involvement in established networks and global forums addressing economic injustice, such as the Micah Network, Micah Challenge, and the Christian Community Development Association, as well as encourage the formation of new networks around this issue.

8. We must seek to incorporate issues related to economic justice into pastoral training, seminary curriculums, weekly preaching and Sunday schools.[14]

9. We must encourage and seek various means of carefully[15] planned exposure of leaders, business people, and influencers to situations of economic injustice.

10. We must document and publish examples, case studies, and projects of Christians addressing economic justice at local and national levels.

11. We encourage the Lausanne movement to use its influence to

---

including many Christian organizations, are serving some 67 million clients worldwide with credit, savings, and other products (S. Daley-Harris, State of the Microcredit Summit Report 2003, Microcredit Summit, New York). Innovations continue to be developed with the hope of serving more clients as well as existing ones better. It must be mentioned, however, that the microfinance movement is not without its criticisms. Many institutions do not serve the poorest of the poor, the most vulnerable. Many clients are only moderately poor, while still vulnerable, actually *non-poor* (J. Sebstad and M. Cohen, *Synthesis Report on Microfinance, Risk Management and Poverty, Assessing the Impact of Microfinance Services [AIMS]*, Washington, D.C., 2000). Also, the vast majority of clients served are less risky urban traders, merchants, and artisans, rather than farmers in rural areas where three-fourths of the poor live.

[14] In particular, we need the promulgation of economic training and tools for the Kingdom to help the church to view business as a blessing, recognizing the positive role of production, jobs, even taxes, and other enterprise creation programs for the Kingdom.

[15] In a way that avoids dehumanizing the poor through exposure trips that further entrench the "us" versus "them" mentality.

promote mainstream media exposure (e.g., *Christianity Today*) to issues of economic justice.

12. We need to resource pastors with sermon outlines, narratives, tapes, discipleship guides on issues related to economic justice and emphasize theological training that addresses issues related to materialism and the prosperity gospel.

13. We must develop, list[16] and distribute information, resources, tools, conference opportunities, books and periodicals related to implementing productive economic activity as a tool for Christian ministry.

14. We need to promote understanding of the negative *ecological* impact of economic injustice.

15. We need to become actors[17] in the public realm to reshape the global economy so that benefits of globalization, for example access to markets, are available to the marginalized and the vulnerable.

16. We need to encourage debt relief, fair trade and the transparency and accountability of governments, transnational corporations, and the international banking sector.

17. We need to challenge and hold NGO's, mission agencies, and Christian businesses accountable for their actions in the realm of economic justice.

18. We need to encourage the church and individual Christians to engage in alternative economics, such as the fair trade movement.

19. The church must encourage discussion on the relationship of economic injustice to terrorism.

---

[16] For example, a bibliography of training resources.
[17] For example, through political engagement, advocacy, speaking, and writing.

20. We must promote awareness, understanding, and engagement at the macro and microlevels of *secular society*, emphasizing a biblical vision as the solution to economic injustice.

DEVELOPMENT IS LIKE A RIVER

Karl J. Franklin

I n this article, by means of parable and personal experiences, I describe some of the problems associated with development in general, and also among the Kewa people of Papua New Guinea (PNG). I use the metaphor of a river to suggest how money flows in development projects, including those fostered by mission agencies. I add a water bottling parable to suggest that cultural assessment and management techniques influence decisions about development needs.

Development as a River

I compare development to a river, with money flowing through it. The river may be deep, with lots of money in it, or it may be broad, so that the money is scattered through the waters. In either case, the money flows along with the water and, as it does, it may flow fast, as when in flood, or slowly, as when it begins to dry up.

Tributaries feed the river, so it usually starts out clean and is a positive agent for transportation, irrigation, food supply, and a habitat for animals. Development projects, including Bible translation and literacy are clean but often depend upon the flow of money in their various stages. In the West, and for much of the world, there is no recognized development unless there is financial investment and capital gain. Both the private sector and government agencies are responsible for how much money flows in the river and how it gets there. The money also starts out clean as the government and private agencies determine its flow. In development philosophies, including capitalism on the one hand

and socialism on the other, the objective is theoretically to help the citizens of the country get help from the river and not drown in it.

When a river is in flood it picks up and carries a lot of debris along with the water. As the waters swell, materials collect from the banks of the river, from tributaries, and from other sources. In disastrous cases, the debris can become so voluminous that it impedes the water and causes a "logjam."

Basically, a person's cultural perspective will influence their interpretation of what they consider as development. In PNG government and private agencies provide aid for health, education, infrastructure, and everything else that flows along with the money. However, people can become frustrated with the process and a log jam can occur, or they build dykes or levees to help repel the flood. Even religious (or non-religious) ideas effect and determine what flows in the river—cargo cults in PNG, for example, arise out of a desire to encourage and sustain a flood of goods and money.[1] Floods of money often inhibit personal and group initiative by those who believe they should help one another vis-à-vis community and individual involvement.

Most enduring development projects, including the "planting" of churches are built around solid community development principles, illustrating the long known principle of Roland Allen's:

> It is of comparatively small importance how the missionary is maintained: it is of comparatively small importance how the

---

[1] The history of cargo cults in the Madang (coastal) area of PNG dates back to Mikloucho-Maclay (see the reference to his diaries at the end of this article). Although old now, the best overall description and summary of cargo cults is by Peter Lawrence (1964). More recently Errington and Gewertz (2004) follow the development of the Ramu sugar plantation, particularly a question by one of the cargo leaders about why the black people have had so little cargo compared to the white people who came to PNG.

finances of the Church are organized: what is of supreme importance is how these arrangements, whatever they may be, affect the minds of the people, and so promote, or hinder, the spread of the Gospel (Allen 1962:49).

Observations on Development

The interest of development agencies in the country and people of Papua New Guinea (PNG) is staggering.[2] My wife and I lived there for over 30 years and for almost half of that time we were closely involved with a particular group of people called the Kewa. We worked in the Eastern dialect and the Western dialect, learning to speak both, so we were well acquainted with the needs and aspirations of the people. The government was also concerned about the welfare of the rural Kewa people (and other groups as well) and tried a number of development projects, which I shall briefly outline.

We began living in the village of Muli (with 400 people, living mainly at an altitude of about 6,000') in the Southern Highlands Province of PNG in 1958 and lived there, for over half of our time, until 1963. The Kewa people are subsistence farmers whose main traditional crop was the sweet potato (*ipomoea batatas*), supplemented by taro, sugar cane, tapioca and bananas.[3] Pigs were domesticated and killed mainly for traditional feasts, or in cases of sickness that required propitiation. In the late 1950s the government agricultural department decided to introduce sheep into the East Kewa area, but eventually rainfall and soil conditions caused foot disease problems and the effort was a failure. In addition, there was no infrastructure or experience to

---

[2] The Directory of Development Organizations 2008: Volume VI/http://www.devdir.org (last accessed March, 2009) has 115 organizations listed, many of them government departments and services. SIL International in PNG, the agency I worked for, is not listed, nor is most missionary agencies.

[3] See Franklin (1991) for a summary of the Kewa people and their culture.

support a wool industry. Later, in the 1970s, government agricultural officers introduced cattle into the West Kewa area and various clans bought them from a commercial enterprise in the Sugu Valley. The people were well acquainted with raising pigs and were anxious to take on the cattle (and previously the sheep) projects. Cattle failed because they were difficult to provide pasture for and they were adept at getting out of pastures and causing havoc in the peoples' gardens. The government agricultural officers had also forbid the people to slaughter cows with the pigs at traditional large feasts.

Another effort tried in the Muli area was the cultivation of pyrethrum, a small daisy-like flower that is used in pesticides. People have to pick and dry the flowers, a difficult task in an area with so much rainfall, then collect them for buyers or take them to a center. The project folded after a short trial period.

There are two other projects that were tried while we lived in the Usa village area of the West Kewa dialect area from 1967 to 1973, with occasional visits after that up until 1990. These were coffee gardens and a large tea plantation. The people continue to grow coffee trees in garden areas around the village, but the tea plantation never was successful. It was too far to get the leaves to the nearest processing factory, some three hours away, even if the roads were passable and there was transportation.

In areas near urban centers there are fresh food markets where the Kewa people sell vegetables, but these are also often centers that allow frequent drinking, playing cards and gambling. Some of the Kewa women sell scones that they bake and net bags that they weave. The Kewa men have developed a basket and tray weaving business and take their products to urban centers or set up stalls along the main roads to sell their wares. I have seen such Kewa products in all the major towns of PNG.

Returning to our analogy of flooding and money, the people retrieved some of the money that flowed in the river for the initial tea project, but the river eventually dried up because there was no sustainable infrastructure—the bridges and banks had collapsed.

A "Development" Parable

"What are we going to do with all those cartons of bottled water sitting on the warehouse shelves"? It was Ankshas Nervonsen speaking, chief executive in charge of the distribution of the Okansa Spring Water. He was referring to 50 cases of natural Okansa, each with 24 bottles, a total of 7,400 perfectly packaged half-pint bottles of pure, sparking water. Ankshas knew that the water was indeed good. It had been carefully harvested and distributed by a team of water experts who knew good water when they saw it and the best way to get it. They had spent years researching the Ozark mountains, studying the terrain, the geology to a depth of 500 feet, methods of hygienic harvesting, and so on. "No," mused Ankshas, "there is nothing wrong with the water on the shelves—there must be some other problem."

The problem was why Ankshas had called his Board together, or rather, why the Board had asked Ankshas for a report on "Water on the Shelves," as they had listed the item on the agenda. He was being questioned by his Board because the Board had been questioned by the funders of Okansa, contributors to the goal of "Every household with natural Okansa by the end of the century." Everyone who read the mission statement assumed it was the present century, but no one had actually said so. "Don't you realize, Ankshas," said the Board chairperson, a woman named Apello Kritensen, "that water on the shelf is a denial to a thirsty person?" Apello was expressing the concern of all the Board and they were relentless in their questions. "Did you do a feasibility study of Clinton County before you sent 100 cases there?" asked one. "Were other water facilitators involved in the action?" asked another. "Why didn't you spend more time teaching people how to drink the water?" mumbled a third.

And so it went for the whole morning. The Board was asking questions and demanding action, which, in the end, meant establishing several committees to study the actions necessary to get the Okansa off the shelves. They also decided to appoint a Vice President responsible for water consumption and distribution. Their goal was to be sure that their actions were not only studied, but done so using effective cost-benefit management tools. And what were the tools they decided to use? In addition to the ubiquitous task force, they outlined symposiums, training groups, workshops, market surveys, promotions, webcasts, and other truly integrated systems. They promised the backing, involvement and support from all vice presidents and area sales managers. They discussed outsource options, but realized quickly that few outsiders knew much about the secrets of Okansa. Therefore they appointed people from within the ranks, who had "been there and done that," to quote one of the Board members.

One of the more illustrious committees that the Board established was the Water-Impact Committee. "We want to know what happens when people drink Okansa," explained Apello. "It's no use just bottling the water, giving out some free samples, even putting a nice colorful label on the bottle—we want to know how this water is changing the community, especially Clinton county for a starter."

Ankshas had his mandate and he also had his committee. He also knew something about bottled water. Before he became the chief executive he had bottled water himself. And he knew that it wasn't easy. You had to find people who knew something about water and work with them. Sure, they might not yet have developed a taste for pure water, but they could learn. Every person has the capacity to discern water that is good and pure from water that is so-so. Ankshas knew that and yet his supervising committee wanted action and they wanted results. "Find out why no one is buying the water—it's not rocket science," one of the Board members had bellowed at him.

It seemed to Ankshas that there could be a number of reasons why people were not buying the water. First of all, at least in

Clinton County, it rained most days and people were simply not thirsty. "You don't sell Eskimos ice cubes or Polynesians fish," Ankshas had retorted, but the analogies to culture were lost on most Board members.

While Ankshas was thinking, the Water Impact Committee got right to work. After purchasing laptop computers and wireless hookups for all the members, the Committee Vice-President got started on his familiarization tour. He visited 53 countries, including Clinton County, and 21 water bottling projects. He racked up 225,000 frequent flyer miles in the process, as well as malaria and three bouts of diarrhea. But it was worth it—in the end he had 9 notebooks of data to share with his Committee.

The Water Impact Committee met with Ankshas on the 15th of May, the first day of the week that the President of the US had proclaimed "Water Watch Week." The imagery and symbolization were important to the work and needs of the committee. The chairman wasted little time in getting to the point: "We have found," he intoned in a solemn and magisterial manner, "that bottled water doesn't sell well in wet climates. However," he reported, "we believe that with better training and more rigid bottling standards we can assure the would-be customers that our water will suit their needs, whether they are thirsty or not."

And so, in due course, The Board established a Water Training Standards Committee that modeled a rigid set of standards for anyone who wished to bottle water. They would be schooled in Latin, geology, hydrology, and water-witching, each subject with professors experienced with water themselves. Not all training would be "up-front"; instead most would be "just in time." And it would be done close to the springs from which the water came. There were other constraints and the Board established review committees to assess the outcomes. In the future, they would leave nothing to chance, nor to the whims of the people who would drink the water.

Epilogue

Fifteen years have passed and the water on the shelves is still there. It is stale now and some of the water project workers think it should be dumped and new water bottles bought. The Water Impact Committee, which now has offices in every continent and most countries, is not so sure. They, however, are willing to study the issue and make formal recommendations to the various committees that collect and analyze the masses of information on hand. We will have to wait and see if Okansa survives.

Summary

David Maranz worked for many years in Africa. He reminds us (2001:199), "I find it is clear that the use of resources, and especially the question of money, is a major concern for virtually every one.... The problems are confusing, pressing, and often distressing... [and that] many who work with Westerners find much of their behavior confusing, unintelligible, or even disagreeable." Unfortunately, development money seems to flow freely, but with continuing cultural misinterpretations.

I have used actual instances and a parable to highlight why some development projects fail. We might feel that the conceptual frameworks of the parties involved were wrong and that failure was, therefore, inevitable. The point is, however, that there is no positive and necessary relationship between the resources of a particular agency and the progress of a project, especially if there is a lot of money floating down the river.

References

Allen, Roland
    1962 [1912]. *Missionary Methods: St. Paul's or Ours?* Grand
        Rapids, MI: Eerdmans Pub.
Errington, Frederick & Deborah Gewertz
    2004. *Yali's Question: Sugar, Culture, and History.* Chicago: The
        University of Chicago Press.

Franklin, Karl J.
> 1991. Kewa. In Terence E. Hays, Volume ed. *Encyclopedia of World Cultures.* Volume II: Oceania. pp. 114-117. Boston: G.K. Hall & Co

Lawrence, Peter
> 1964. *Road Belong Cargo: A Study of the Cargo Movement in the Southern Madang District New Guinea.* Melbourne: Melbourne University Press.

Maanz, David E.
> 2001. *African Friends and Money Matters: Observations from Africa. Dallas,* TX: SIL International and International Museum of Cultures.

Mikloucho-Maclay
> *New Guinea Diaries 1871-1883.* Madang: Kristen Pres.
>> [Translated from the Russian with biographical comments by C.L. Sentinella.]

Raising Up a New Generation from the 4/14 Window to Transform the World

Luis Bush

You have established a stronghold from the mouths of children and nursing infants...to silence the enemy and the avenger.

– Psalm 8:2 (HCSB)[1]

At the end of the last century I wrote a pamphlet entitled *The 10/40 Window: Getting to the Core of the Core.*[2] In the first years of this new century, I am urging a new missional focus: the 4/14 Window. Although in a different sense, it too can be called "the core of the core." The 10/40 Window referenced a geographic frame; the 4/14 Window describes a demographic frame—a life season comprising the ten years between the ages of 4 and 14.

This chapter is an urgent appeal to consider the strategic importance and potential of the 1.2 billion children and youth in the 4/14 Window. It is a plea to open your heart and mind to the idea of reaching and raising up a new generation from within that vast group—a generation that *can* experience personal transformation and *can* be mobilized as agents for transformation throughout the world. Our vision and hope is to maximize their transformational impact while they are young, and to mobilize them for continuing impact for the rest of their lives. I invite you to join with many others who are making a commitment to fulfill this vision and realize this hope.

To maximize the transformational impact of children and youth in the 4/14 Window we must address the spiritual, mental, physical, relational, economic, and social issues they face. We must also confront their "ministerial poverty"—the scarcity of opportunities for them to exercise their gifts and achieve their potential in ways that honor God and advance His Kingdom.

It is crucial that mission efforts be re-prioritized and re-directed toward the 4/14 age group worldwide. This requires that we become acutely aware of what is taking place in their lives. We must also endeavor to understand their nature and the essential means to nurture them. Only with this kind of informed awareness will we be able to reach them, shape them, and raise them up to transform the world.

This chapter presents an overview of the needs, nature and potential of children and youth in the 4/14 Window. It also addresses the very real opposition and obstacles to raising them up as a transformational generation. We must not be defeated by the opposition or deterred by the obstacles; and as we engage in strategic global thinking and answer God's call to catalytic action, we must do so within a biblical framework.

Scripture makes it absolutely clear that the transformational mission of God involves bringing together all things under the headship of Christ (Ephesians 1:9-10) through the church, which is His body. The church is the fullness of Christ on earth, who fills all in all (Ephesians 1:22-23), with the result that all things on earth are reconciled and aligned to Him (Colossians 1:20).The body of Christ worldwide—including children and youth in the 4/14 Window—are God's agents of transformation under the headship of Jesus Christ. Every Christ follower in every community and nation—even children and youth—are called to involvement in Christ's transformational mission.

As we approach this bold initiative, engaging and seeking to equip a new generation to transform the world, we do well to adopt the watchword, "transformed and always transforming." This simple phrase reminds us that transformation is a process and is not fully realized until Jesus comes again. We are co-laborers with Christ, under His headship, collaborating with Him in His transformational mission to raise up a new generation from the 4/14 Window to transform the world.

Such global transformation will only take place as God's people are individually re-made through the renewing of their minds (Romans 12:1-2). Then they will discover the good and perfect will of God, this will be their "spiritual act of worship," and they will be led to engage in God's mission.

The 4/14 Window: Ages of Opportunity and Challenge

In human development there is no more critical period than the decade represented by the 4/14 Window. It is a profoundly formative period when perspectives are shaped either positively or negatively and when a view of one's own significance (or lack of significance) is formulated. The needs and potential of this age group should inspire a purposeful response by those charged today with forming the world of tomorrow. It is a call to turn "the hearts of the fathers to their children and the hearts of the children to their fathers" (Malachi 4:6).

The Intersection of the 10/40 Window and the 4/14 Window

In 2008, fifteen years into a worldwide mission emphasis on the 10/40 Window, there are encouraging indicators that this has been a region highly responsive to the presentation of the Gospel. The annual growth rate of Christ followers in the 10/40 Window was almost twice that of those outside the 10/40 Window.[4] Christ followers in the 10/40 Window nations increased from 2.5% of the population in 1990 to 4.7% in 2005. The general population grew at only 1.5% annually, while the population of Christ followers grew at an amazing 5.4% per year![5]

If we correlate these statistics with the fact that almost 70% of the world's 4- to 14-year olds (833,378,750) live in the 10/40 Window, we can begin to see the intersection of the 10/40 and the 4/14 Window.[6] The 10/40 Window is the geographical area with the greatest need and opportunity. The 4/14 Window is the demographical grouping that is the most open, receptive, and moldable to every form of spiritual and developmental input.

The most compelling conclusion regarding the relationship between the 10/40 and the 4/14 windows is that efforts be refocused on *the 4/14 within the 10/40* in order to reach the most receptive persons in the area of the greatest need and opportunity. In so doing we are also recognizing the importance of children and youth in God's work of transforming the world.

When he was asked by His disciples "Who, then, is the greatest in the kingdom of heaven?" Jesus called a little child, whom he placed among them. And He said: "Truly I tell you, unless you change and become like little children, you will never enter the kingdom of heaven. Therefore, whoever takes a humble place—becoming like this child—is the greatest in the kingdom of heaven. And whoever welcomes one such child in my name welcomes me. If anyone causes one of these little ones—those who believe in me—to stumble, it would be better for them if a large millstone were hung around their neck and they were drowned in the depths of the sea"(Matthew 18:1-6 TNIV).

Have we really listened to Jesus' teaching about the place of children in the kingdom of God? First, they model the essence of gospel faith and faithful discipleship by showing us how to humbly repent and to trust in the God of salvation. Second, to 'welcome' a child—that is, to accept, love, value and respect a child—is to welcome Christ Himself! Finally, as Jesus made very clear, whoever neglects, abuses, hinders, or turns away a child from faith in Christ will face severe judgment from God Himself.

The 4/14 Age Group Around the World

A country-by-country comparison of the nations with the most 4-to-14ers is revealing. India, with almost 20% fewer people than China, has over 30% more children and youth. This is largely due to China's infamous "one child" policy. Nigeria and Indonesia, with half the population of the U.S., actually have more children and young teens in absolute numbers. In the U.S., 25% of the nearly 42 million school-age children are Hispanic—though Hispanics comprise only 15% of the general population. It is important to note that in Africa and in places such as Gaza, Afghanistan, Pakistan and most Middle Eastern countries, 40 to 50% of the population is under 15 years of age.[7]

Contrast this with the countries with the lowest percentage of persons under age 15—Italy (13.8%), Japan (14.3%), Germany (14.4%),[8] etc. It can be readily seen that by far the greatest population growth is taking place in the least developed and often most conflicted countries of the world.

Characteristics of the 4/14 Window

The world's 4 to 14-year-olds present us with several pressing realities. The 4/14 years represent a "season of awakening" in which a person's understanding of life emerges and one's conscience is awakened to judge right from wrong. But the life circumstances of today's typical 4/14er is a cross between a minefield and an obstacle course.

A disturbing number of 4/14ers in the 10/40 Window are condemned to a life of serfdom, brutal labor, sexual exploitation, spiritual oppression and emotional abuse. Most of those exiting the 4/14 Window quickly leave behind their parents' supervision. When formal schooling ends they either enter the work force to make ends meet or further their education in an environment fraught with the dangers of secular ideology and materialism.

Parents and older siblings serve as the most potent and positive influence for many 4/14ers. But sadly, for many others, parents are negligent and siblings are morally damaging. This is especially true when those older brothers and sisters are themselves adversely influenced by today's toxic youth cultures.

While challenges and pitfalls abound, and the pessimism of many adults is amply warranted, the possibilities and potential of 4/14ers is astonishing. For many, the tendency has been to ignore or dismiss their potential or to view those in the 4 to 14 age group as a nagging problem to be endured. We have often failed to grasp the inestimable value of these young lives, made in the image of God. Most significantly, we have failed to recognize that most people who will ever make a decision to follow Christ will do so during the critical years between the ages of 4 and 14.

From a missions standpoint, our interest in the 4 to 14 age group is not only because they are the most *receptive*, but also because as we will see, they are often the most *effective* agents for mission. Of course, Jesus understood their worth: "I praise you Father, Lord of heaven and earth," He said, "because you have hidden these things from the wise and learned, and revealed them to little children. Yes, Father, for this was your good pleasure" (Matthew 11:25-26).

In a three-year project called *The Child in Law, Religion and Society*, researchers examined the so-called mystery of the child. Their final report urges readers to reject the prevalent view that a child is a problem to be controlled. Instead, the authors contend, adults ought to nurture wonder in children while seeking their own "childlikeness," or "childness." They warn against the fallacy of reductionism, the philosophy that attempts to reduce a complex system to the sum of its parts. In this case, reductionism endeavors to categorize a child through various problematic elements; for example, the incidence of delinquency, abuse or autism. Some reductionists have gone so far as to define a child as "the sum of neuron firings in the brain" or "nothing but a victim of original sin."[10] Such thinking demeans the wondrous, mysterious nature of childhood—a mystery that is rooted in the Scriptures, particularly in the words of Jesus.

Christ is the King of the Kingdom, and the faith of the child is the model for all who would enter and live out their lives in the Kingdom with King Jesus. The Gospel elevates children to a very high place of honor in the Kingdom and gives them moral agency. Children are addressed as responsible members of the family of God, as those who are "in the Lord" (Ephesians 6:1).

It is imperative that we see children and young people as a crucial, strategic force that can transform a generation and change the world. Speaking of children, Jesus said, "to such belongs the kingdom of God" (Luke 18:16). Clearly, from the time of the first disciples (Mark 10:13-16) to the present day, we have often underestimated the value and potential of children. Time and again, we have failed to effectively and strategically reach them. The challenge before us is to raise up today's 4- to 14-year olds to experience the abundant life Jesus promised (John 10:10b), to free them from spiritual, mental, physical, relational, economic, social, and ministerial poverty, to harness their immense potential, and to deploy them to change the world.

The Modern Context of the 4/14ers
The 4/14ers (and their older siblings) are called the "Internet Generation" because the Net is their primary influencer. While their parents are digital immigrants, the world's children and young people are digitally native. They are less defined by geography than by technology.

It is true that there are still parts of the world where the Internet does not yet have a major culture-shaping role, due to lack of accessibility. However, with the shrinking of the "global village," more and more young people in remote areas will become connected and correspondingly influenced by the culture of western materialism and hedonism.

Today's children and young people have been given a host of labels such as "Digital kids," "Millennials" or "Mosaics." These labels suggest that today's kids are vastly different in culture and worldview from the Baby Boomer era. They are living in a postmodern age where the spirit of deconstructionism is pecking away at their values, affecting their self-identity and changing their view of the home, school, and society at large.[20]

Today's young people are "Facebookers" and "YouTubers" who do not think twice about sharing their opinions online with strangers whom they call "friends." Technology provides them with a powerful weapon to bring change, but it is also a powerful poison that can bring destruction. This generation wants their opinions to be heard and they want to make a difference. They are creative and speak openly of their feelings.[21]

The 4/14ers are riding a technological wave in to the future. More than any previous generation, they are plugged in—all the time—with a world of communication and information at their fingertips. "The youth of today, due to the strong influence of technology in their everyday lives, are constantly confronted with the problem of self-definition. To most adolescents, technologies such as mobile phones are implicated in the production of individuality and personhood.[22]

Traditional values face unprecedented challenges in the digital world. The Internet provides youth the world over with instant access to a wide variety of cultural styles, and "McWorld" values and the technological culture reaches around the world, replacing even long-held values. India, for example, is a nation where communication technology has produced dramatic changes in youth culture resulting in a drastic decline in traditional values. India exemplifies the global youth culture phenomenon. The revolutionary information age is widening social distances, weakening family ties and changing the child-parent relationship.

The World Values Survey[23] findings accentuate the conclusion that intergenerational changes are taking place in basic values related to politics, applied economics, religion, gender roles, family and sexual norms. The values of younger generations differ consistently from those prevailing among older generations, and are transforming social, economic, and political life; in some cases displacing thousands of years of traditional cultures in the span of a single generation.

There is much that is frightening and disheartening in the exposure and "flatness" in this "brave new world." As uncomfortable as we in the older generations might be in the Internet culture, it is undeniable that the 4/14ers are very much at home there, and will be ever more so as it continues to unfold at unprecedented pace. However, we must understand and accept that this very connectedness and instant information access and sharing is part of the great potential of the 4/14ers to transform their world.

The Challenge: Maximizing Transformational Impact in the 4/14 Age Group

Any sensible parent knows the childhood years are formative. Anyone who has been a child knows it too! Our brains are 90% formed before we reach the age of three[24] and 85% of our adult personality is formed by the time we reach six years of age. There is substantial truth in the Jesuits' refrain, "Show me a child when he is seven and I'll show you the man." A biblical proverb attributed to King Solomon, the wisest man who ever lived, instructs us, "Train up a child in the way he should go; even when he is old he will not depart from it" (Proverbs 22:6). In light of that truth, our task is to "train up" the 4/14 generation in the way they should go, so that as they grow older they will be used by God to transform the world.

This is a multi-faceted challenge we face, and it can be met only with a holistic approach. In raising up the 4/14 generation for transformational impact, we must address their physical needs (especially the physical needs of those in poverty), their intellectual needs, and all the relational, social and spiritual dimensions of their lives. We must embrace the whole person, endeavoring to see 4/14ers as God sees them. In relating to those who live in impoverished conditions we must look beyond the lack of assets and advantages and see the complete individual. We must also recognize the cyclical, negative forces at work. Jayakumar Christian, a leader with World Vision in India, describes poverty as a set of disempowering systems that result in ongoing or even intensified poverty.[25] These exploitative systems interact with each other to supplant the role of God in the lives of the poor. This results in the development of god-like structures that oppress people and produce a distorted view of God. Cultural systems legitimize these god-complexes and reinforce the distortions. All of these systems are based on deception and lies about who people really are and who God really is. They systematically victimize people who are made in the image of God, exchanging the truth for a lie and causing people to worship and serve created things rather than the Creator. (See Romans 1:25).

As a result of their marred identities and vocational insecurities, the poor believe that they were born to be oppressed. They also conclude that they have nothing to offer, and the negative self identity becomes a self-fulfilling prophecy. The non-poor, on the other hand, often believe that they have the right to exploit and enjoy the fruits of the poor's labor. As long as these core perspectives remain in effect, a fatalistic mindset will lock the poor into their poverty. What is true of the entire world's poor is especially true of the children and youth whose lives are molded and futures cast during the 4/14 years.

The 4/14 Window is the first point of access to reverse the systematic lies of culture and remake a generation through holistic development. Let's examine each of seven basic challenges we encounter in the 4/14 Window.

1. The Spiritual Challenge

As noted previously, most people who will ever make a decision to follow Christ will do so before their 15th birthday. In the

USA, nearly 85% of people who make a decision for Christ, do so between the ages of 4 and 14.[26] During the 20th century, that age group was the single largest source of new believers for the American church.

In his book *Transforming Your Children into Spiritual Champions*,[27] George Barna presents the results of three years of research that confirm that timeless principle from the wisdom literature: "Train up a child in the way he should go; even when he is old he will not depart from it" (Proverbs 22:6 ESV).

Barna's research verifies that a person's lifelong behaviors and beliefs are generally developed during childhood and early adolescence. In the overwhelming majority, most of the moral and spiritual foundations are in place by age nine. Fundamental perspectives on truth, integrity, meaning, justice, morality, and ethics are formed at this early stage of life.

In the 4/14 age group we also see the natural confluence of evangelism and discipleship. Barna observes, "By the age of 13, one's spiritual identity is largely set in place."[29] If we can reach children and youth and disciple them when their life perspectives and worldviews are being shaped, we will set them on a rock that cannot be easily moved.

These statistics reveal a vast spiritual harvest waiting to be reaped. For too long, the ministries of most churches, Christian organizations and mission agencies have focused primarily on adults, with fewer personnel, minimal funds, and limited creativity devoted to young people and to children. In no way should we abandon the outreach to any age group, but the call of the 4/14 initiative is clear: We must prioritize our efforts to reach the world's largest, most receptive and most moldable group—the 4 to 14-year-olds.

Admittedly, focusing on the 4/14ers is a challenge more easily met in some nations than in others. However, just because children tend to be receptive to the Gospel does not mean that we can be carefree in how we approach them or their parents. Indeed, that heightened receptivity should cause us to be even more cautious and discerning, for the possibility of exploitation or abuse is also heightened.

Cross-cultural missionaries must study the cultures and the contexts of the adult peoples to whom they minister. The same applies to those who would do inter-faith "mission" among children. When ministering to children, the servant of Christ must be wise, sensitive, cautious, discerning and holistic in reaching out to those from non-Christian contexts.

In 2008, the Global Children's Forum (GCF) was formed. The GCF is a partnership of children's ministry agencies that operate on a global or regional basis. Its focus is on the strategic need for evangelism and discipleship among the world's two billion children. Its goal is to ensure that every child is given the opportunity to know who Jesus is, what He offers and how to know Him personally.

The Outcome of Spiritual Transformation Brings Community Transformation through the Presence of God at Work in and through His People

The heart of transformation is the transformation of the heart. The central need is spiritual in nature. This is clear from God's Word where He reveals His perfect plan to reverse the effects of the fall on His creation. Spiritual transformation does not only mean the forgiveness of sins; it encompasses all of life, recreated by God. The spiritual transformation of the individual through the power of the Gospel therefore provides the platform upon which all the spheres of society can be transformed.

By transformation we do not mean behavior modification or a striving to "make the world a better place." Transformation entails a passionate seeking after God, submitting to His transforming power and allowing Him to realign every facet of our lives according to His design and plan.

Although God desires to transform each individual, there is also a communal component to transformation—the Body of Christ, a community comprising individuals who have been transformed by the Gospel. The Body of Christ is the place where societal transformation begins and from which individuals emerge as agents of transformation in their various spheres of influence.

2. The Mental/Cognitive Challenge

By the time the typical child reaches age nine, the mental gears are shifted and the child begins to use internal cues to either confirm or challenge an existing perspective. As the child grows into adolescence, change becomes more and more difficult. By adulthood, only with great effort or under great influence will a person replace existing views and understandings. George Barna notes that "adults essentially carry out the beliefs they embraced when they were young."[30] This view challenges the stages of intellectual development[31] formulated by Jean Piaget, et. al., contending that one must reach the age of 15 to be capable of reasoning as an adult.

Every mature society recognizes childhood and adolescence as a time to prepare the young for the remainder of life. Most often this is done through the establishment of primary and secondary schools. Educators worldwide understand the critical importance of the 4/14 Window in the correct formation of children; however, despite the efforts of many governments, untold millions of children receive little or no education. This problem of substandard education is exacerbated by other factors—the disintegration of the family unit, poverty, ill health, poor nutrition, to name but a few. This then results in masses of unmotivated, poorly educated men and women, barely capable of earning a meager income. And the situation is further complicated for children whose own parents deprive them of an education by forcing them to work in order to help support the family.

The Need for a Transformational Approach to Education

While universal primary and secondary education may be considered a worthy goal, its ultimate effect is often negative.

Unless the teachers and those who run the schools are Christ followers, the worldview that is taught will not transform the minds of the 4/14ers to be able to test and approve what God's will is for them (Romans 12:1-2). A further complication is that childhood education in many countries has been taken away from the jurisdiction of the parents and the church.

Secular education does not enlighten; rather, it dims one's grasp of the "real reality" acknowledged in the truth of Scripture. It seeks to remove the notion that God exists or that we owe allegiance to a Creator.[32] Naturalistic worldviews and rationalism in secular education have conspired to predispose against the supernatural, even to despise it. By forcing children to be taught a curriculum that robs God of his rightful preeminence, such educational systems are sabotaging the blessing of Jesus who "came that they may have life, and have it abundantly."

Godless, secular indoctrination is an age-old problem, one that we see described in the Bible. Consider the experience of Daniel and his three friends (Daniel 1). They were only boys, 11-14 years old, taken from their parents and shipped off to pagan Babylon. Their captors even gave them new names—a practice that continues in Christless authoritarian systems to this day. What happened to Daniel and his friends was like the name changes given to local residents on the Korean peninsula at the beginning of the 20th century and just a few years later in the Soviet Union after the Communist Revolution. The four boys in Babylon were given heathen names in replacement for their covenantal names associated with the one only true God.

The plan was to subtly win them for Babylon, to transform their minds until they were completely captivated by the Babylonian thought forms, worldview, culture, religion and way of life. The Babylonian system of public education with its goal of a pervasive secularism reminds of us of government-run public educational systems in our world today. But all of the attempts at mind control and behavior modification failed miserably. Daniel and his friends did not forget their early God-centered education;

they did not lose their faith; they would not be robbed of trust in the one true God.

As we consider the public education systems in our nations at the beginning of the 21ˢᵗ century, we must find encouragement from the Book of Daniel that God is supreme, that He is in control, that He can be trusted. More than once, the worldly king of Babylon, the feared Nebuchadnezzar, was moved to declare about God, "His kingdom is an eternal kingdom; his dominion endures from generation to generation" (Dan 4:3, 34). Through his own trial as a result of denying the God of the universe, King Nebuchadnezzar ultimately delivered this edict: "I issue a decree requiring that in every part of the kingdom people must fear and reverence the God of Daniel. For he is the living God and he endures forever; his kingdom will not be destroyed, his dominion will never end" (Daniel 6:26).

We can learn today from those who have gone before us—from Daniel and his friends, from educators like Augustine, and from others who stayed faithful in pursuit of God's purposes. A transformational approach to education begins with the premise that all truth is God's truth. The legacy of St. Augustine is that it is the duty of the Christian to learn as much as possible about as many things as possible including scientific inquiry and the pursuit of knowledge and of beauty, recognizing that God is the ultimate source of all truth and all beauty.

Therefore we encourage parents and their children to be discerning in what they learn in whatever educational context to reject what is anti-Christian, to accept and use what is true, and through the Gospel to transform "secular" knowledge and culture into serviceable "Egyptian gold" to serve and worship God (Exodus 35:20-29).

The Outcome of the Transformation of the Mind is the Transformation of the Culture and Nation

Like Daniel, the renewing or metamorphosis of the mind (Rom 12:1-2) can result in the transformation of the culture. The manifesto of a new influential school of thought on human progress and nation building is called *Culture Matters: How Values Shape Human Progress*, by Samuel P. Huntington and Lawrence E. Harrison.[33] These scholars ponder the question of why, at the beginning of the 21st century, the world is more divided than ever between the rich and the poor, between those living in freedom and those under oppression. The concluding thought summarizes their findings: Cultural values shape the development of nations. It offers an important insight into why some countries and ethnic/religious groups have done better than others, not just in economic terms, but also with respect to consolidation of democratic institutions and social justice. Former Singaporean Prime Minister, Lee Kuan Yew said, "More than economics, more than politics, a nation's culture will determine its fate."[34] In our world there is no greater example of two nations which share the same family roots yet have found two totally different cultures and fates than North and South Korea.

3. The Physical/Health Challenge

A primary measure of human well-being is the Under-5 Mortality Rate—an indispensable gauge of children's health for NGOs around the world. (See *State of the World's Children Report for 2008 by UNICEF.*)

One of the motivations for focusing on children is that more so than any other segment of society, the world's children are suffering, often as a result of the sins of adults. Key statistics reveal the critical nature of this problem:

- More than 91 million children under 5 suffer from debilitating hunger[36]
- 15 million children are orphaned as a result of AIDS[37]
- 265 million children have not been immunized against any disease[38]

Health interventions during childhood can prevent damage that is virtually impossible to repair later in life. Addressing the physical and emotional health issues of the young can result in significant advances in lifelong well-being and personal development. Working to improve the health of children not only provides them a more promising future, it is also an invaluable opportunity to minister to their families and communities. In fact, strategic efforts to improve children's health can lead to the stability of an entire nation.

Where do we begin to address this problem? One of the principal solutions is through the establishment of a biblical worldview.

4. The Economic Challenge—the Physically Poor

The physical health needs of children and youth are closely related to the broader problems of poverty. The staggering reality is that more than one billion of the world's children—56%—are living in poverty or severe deprivation![41] A stunning 37% of the world's children—more than 674 million[42]—live in absolute poverty. Additionally, children living in what is defined as "severe deprivation" struggle with a "lack of income and productive resources to ensure sustainable livelihoods." They are also victims of "hunger and malnutrition, ill health, limited access or lack of access to education and other basic services, increased morbidity and mortality from illness, homelessness and inadequate housing, unsafe environments, social discrimination and exclusion."[43]

Raising up a new generation from the 4/14 Window to transform the world demands that we address the physically poor among the 4/14ers.

- Over one-third of children have to live in dwellings with more than five people per room
- 134 million children have no access to any school whatsoever
- Over half a billion children have no toilet facilities whatsoever
- Almost half a billion children lack access to published information of any kind

- 376 million children have more than a 15-minutewalk to water and/or are using unsafe watersources.[44]

Of special concern amongst the poor in the 4/14 window are the millions of orphans. Indeed, God makes them His own special concern throughout Scripture, so His concern must be ours as well. The overwhelming lack of one-on-one holistic care for orphans makes them one of the most neglected groups in the 4/14 Window.

According to the World Health Organization, 85 percent of the world's orphans are between the ages of 4 and 14. Orphaned girls are "easy targets" for sexual exploitation, due in part to a lowered self-image, loss of family structure, and psychological distress. Orphaned boys within the 4/14 Window often turn to crime, drugs, and are prone to become abusive in adult relationships. This is largely the result of an absence of male leadership, mentorship or protection. In many nations they are easy prey for evil men who bully them into forced labor or recruit them for participation in rebel armies (groups that find abandoned children to be easy fodder to fuel their separatist agendas). According to the Coalition to Stop the Use of Child Soldiers, at least 300,000 children, many as young as 10 years of age, are currently participating as "child soldiers" in armed conflicts around the world.

The Outcome of the Transformation of the Poverty of a Nation
The outcome of God's transforming power in a nation occurs as God's people are reconciled and raised up to fulfill His purposes in building a nation. For the term *transformation* to be properly applied to a community, change must be evident not only in the lives of its inhabitants, but also in the fabric of its institutions. Its people must have sufficient health to work productively; they must have sufficient resources to meet basic needs and live above the level of deprivation and poverty. "A transformed community emerges when both the people and institutions have been overrun by the Kingdom ofGod."[45] The river of life begins to

flow in the communities where death has reigned and the result is the healing of the nation (Revelation 22).

5. The Relational Challenge

Most of us are aware of these and other telling statistics about the needs of poor children around the world. But the fact is that it is not just poor children who are at risk. Actually, all children are at risk. Millions are at risk from poverty, but millions are also at risk from prosperity! Many children and young people today have everything to live with, but nothing to live for.[47] At the deepest level, poverty is what happens to people whose relationships do not work for their well being. A person's well-being is rooted in wholesome relationships.

The Outcome of a Biblical Worldview is the Transformation of the Relationships in a Nation, Resulting in Shalom Communities

Transformation involves seeking positive change in the whole of human life materially, socially and spiritually, by recovering our true identity as human beings created in the image of God and discovering our true vocation as productive stewards, faithfully caring for our world and people.[49] This description of transformation addresses the core issues of identity and vocation.

Restoration of human relationships is rooted in one's spiritual relationship with God. This will result in shalom communities which are the visible fruit of a transformed world. They begin in the home, for at the heart of our earthly existence are family relationships. OneHope has observed a dominant global trend of decaying family relationships, specifically associated with the problem of absentee fathers. There has never been a more glaring need for turning the hearts of the fathers toward their children.[50]

6. The Social Challenge

Children and young adolescents can contribute much to positive social change. What often prevents this from occurring is an absence of adults who believe in them; as a consequence, many

4/14ers do not believe in themselves. Nevertheless, most children and young people respond well to challenges and can participate in opportunities to better their surroundings and their societies.

It is unfortunate that today's 4/14ers are too often sheltered from such challenges and not given opportunities to use and develop their gifts. Many adults have a mistaken idea that children are stressed out, and so should not be "burdened" with additional responsibilities. But, as William Damon, author of the book *Greater Expectations*, reminds us,

> contrary to what some adults think, they really do not need to come home after their six-hour day and 'cool out' in front of the TV. They do need to have their energies fully and joyfully engaged in worthwhile pursuits. Stress for a child is not a function of keeping busy; rather, it is a function of receiving conflicting messages about the self and experiencing troublesome life events beyond one's control. Activities that children gain satisfaction from, and accomplishments that children are proud of, relieve rather than induce stress. Activities that provide genuine services to others are ideal in this regard.[51]

The fact is that where children and young people are given a significant challenge, intentionally by wise adults or "accidentally" through necessity or disaster or obligation, children usually readily adapt to such demands. Given such challenges, Damon notes that children have always "pitched in with energy and pride, with all the natural vigor of childhood. Such experiences gave these children invaluable opportunities to learn personal and social responsibility. In an old-fashioned phrase, they were character-building experiences."[52]

William Damon continues,

> In systematically underestimating the child's capabilities, we are limiting the child's potential for growth. In withholding from children the expectation to serve others...we are preventing them from acquiring a sense of social and personal responsibility. We are leaving the child to dwell on nothing

more noble than gratifying the self's moment-by-moment inclinations. In the end, this orientation is a particularly unsatisfying form of self-centeredness, because it creates a focus on a personal self that has no special skills or valued services to offer anyone else. Paradoxically, by giving the child purposes that go beyond the self, an orientation to service results in a more secure belief in oneself.[53]

7. The Ministry Challenge

The ministry challenge is about encouraging and equipping the children and youth of the 4/14 Window to use their gifts and potential as agents in transforming the world. They represent an enormous untapped pool of influencers with sensitivity to the voice of God and willingness to do His bidding. We need to understand again that God can and does use children and young people—their prayers, their insights, their hands and their feet—in changing the hearts of mankind.

The 4/14ers have great capacity to understand the faith, and great courage and effectiveness as they share their faith. Adults will fail the 4/14ers if they fail to equip them with the vision and opportunity to do something beyond themselves. Indeed, many churches discourage children and young people from finding and developing their natural gifts and aptitudes for character and competence in areas like missions awareness.

Much (most?) of what goes on for children in our churches today is geared to entertaining them rather than equipping or challenging them. It is OK for children and youth to have fun. But there are missed opportunities in making that the focus. We must ask, what are our children not doing and learning while they are being entertained?

Alex and Brett Harris, two 19-year-olds, have written a book called *Do Hard Things*. The Harris boys note that "Being considered a good teen only requires that we don't do bad stuff like taking drugs, drinking and partying. But is it enough to know of the negative things we don't do?"[58]

The 4/14ers thrive on challenges. Children and young teens love opportunities to gain skills and to prove themselves. Generally they respond with energy and enthusiasm when provided opportunities to test their abilities. When denied such challenges, they can become insecure and apathetic.[59] And could there be a more exciting and life-changing challenge than learning about the world, sharing God's love for the peoples of the world and transforming a generation?

Let us not forget that 4/14ers are capable of engaging in spiritual warfare. They have great capacity for fighting spiritual battles through their child-like faith. Certainly, God is no respecter of persons! He can anoint children with the Holy Spirit just as He empowered the apostle Paul and the disciples. Children are sensitive to the Holy Spirit's leading because they have not yet developed the spiritual barriers that many adults have erected over the course of their lives.

The Outcome of Ministering Children Is Increased Faith in God, Answered Prayer and Shalom Communities

Some have stopped to consider the spiritual life and capacity to minister that is within a child. One of these is Robert Coles, who writes about it in *The Spiritual Life of Children*. He provides overwhelming anecdotal evidence that children connect with God on many levels.[62] Coles notes that the discovery of what may lie within a child's spiritual being is rewarding for the adult who listens carefully. The way a child talks about God and the world has an innocence and purity to it that is often lost by adults in this age of multi-tasking.

The potential for children engaged in the ministry of prayer cannot be underestimated. John Robb, chairman of the International Prayer Council and the Children's Prayer Network, believes that some of the praying children of today will become rulers of nations. Many more will be influential for Christ in their generation, bringing His transformation to our world. There is a window of spiritual receptivity in children between the ages of 4-14. Like Samuel, they have a greater openness to hearing God's voice and this is the time to nurture them and invest in their future. After age 14, it can be much harder for them to come to Christ and to give their lives to Him for His purposes on earth.

It is the clear testimony of Scripture that God has chosen to work in human history through the intercessory prayers of His people—including children. In fact, children may be the most powerful source of prayer for community and national transformation.

Psalm 8:2 says that there is power in the prayers and praise of children, "From the lips of children and infants you have ordained praise because of your enemies, to silence the foe and the avenger."

Robb comments, "Our work with children is all about introducing them to a life of intimacy with the Lord through prayer. Prayer is the way we relate directly to God so this work is fulfilling Jesus' command to enable children to come into relationship with Him, a relationship that will change their lives and transform the world around them.

Jesus loved to have children around Him. Roy Zuck notes that "While few of the world's religious leaders have had regard for children, Jesus was different. Not only did He welcome them; He even used them to teach adults some essential spiritual lessons!"[63]

Those who angered Jesus were not just the Pharisees and the vendors in the temple, but also the disciples. On one occasion Jesus became "indignant" when they considered children too unimportant to warrant his attention.[64] Might He also be indignant with those who are negligent and indifferent to the world's children today?

Models of Holistic Approaches for Transformational Development

Transformational Development is a process by which people become whole. It is characterized by growth, change and learning. It is a process of becoming. The direction of development is always toward completeness. As Dan Brewster notes,

> It is not enough to improve only one dimension of a person's life and leave other dimensions in inadequacy. To treat parasitic infection is noble. But if a treated child is left in an unsanitary environment with contaminated water, the intervention is incomplete. If a child receives an education, but social structures prevent him from getting a job, the intervention is incomplete. If a person is introduced to faith in Christ and enjoys spiritual freedom but is left in poverty and oppression, the intervention is incomplete. The scope of development is toward completeness.[65]

Luke 2:52 provides a model for the kind of development involved in the 4/14 vision. This verse simply says, "Jesus grew in wisdom and stature and in favor with God and men." It cites four pivotal components (wisdom, stature, favor with God, and favor with man) and it neatly encompasses all aspects of the whole person and provides a useful model around which one can create meaningful programs that produce holistic development. Our objective through holistic, Christian development is for every child to have the opportunity to grow and develop in each of these areas: in wisdom, in stature, and in favor with God and man.

One example of a holistic approach is that of World Vision International, as described by Jaisankar Sarma, International Director of TransformationDevelopment.[66] The ministry focus is on bringing justice to the poor and the needy; and of the poor and the needy, none is more poor and needy than the child.

World Vision International has prioritized transformational impact in order to affect the whole child, producing well being in each of the child's developmental areas. For instance, again using Luke

2:52as the starting point, a child might grow in stature but if the child doesn't grow in wisdom, then he or she will be incapable of living a productive and meaningful life. A child who grows in wisdom, stature, and favor with man will be spiritually bankrupt if not led to favor with God. Holism is the process by which one experiences the "fullness of life" that Jesus described in John 10:10.

Sarma's definition of "transformational development" involves a process through which children, families, and communities move toward wholeness of life which brings dignity, justice, peace, and hope.[67] The scope of transformational development is wide, including economic, political, environmental, social, and spiritual aspects of life at the local, national, regional, and global levels.

Human transformation, according to Sarma, is a continuous process of profound and holistic change brought about, ultimately, by the work of God. The process and the impact of transformational development are never being divorced from the principles and values of the Kingdom of God.

Transformational development is evidenced by:
- The well-being of girls, boys, families, and communities.
- The empowerment of all girls and boys as agents of transformation themselves.
- The restoration of relationships.
- Communities that are interdependent and empowered.
- Transformed social systems and structures that will empower another generation to begin within the transformed culture.

In the second domain of change, girls and boys participate in the development process in an age-appropriate manner, preparing them to be agents of transformation in their families and communities both in the present and in the future.

These community-based transformational indicators serve as key measures, derived from the transformational framework in the illustration to the right. They provide a helpful, quantifiable basis for assessing impact in programs that seek transformational development—as shown in the chart. This rubric tells us whether our programs and processes are successfully meeting their goals.

The ConneXions Model for Healthy Leadership Development

Within the greater holistic approach a particular emphasis is needed toward holistic spiritual transformation and the development of healthy leaders from an early age. The ConneXions model of healthy leader development provides a Christ-centered set of working principles.[68] It is a framework for life transformation that is widely applicable to the spiritual aspect of the transformation required to reach the 4/14 age group.

Our goal should be nothing less than the entire transformation of the lives of children as they are nurtured in five specific areas of life: Christ, Community, Character, Calling and Competencies. Children first, by faith, come to know God (Christ) because union with Christ is the first and foremost aspect of life transformation. Their union with Christ is encouraged and strengthened through living and growing in a supportive and accountable family, surrogate family and/or church (Community). Within the context of life in community, they grow in integrity (Character), and they are prepared to discover God's purpose for their life (Calling). Finally, they are nurtured to grow in their biblical knowledge, overall education and life skills so that they might fulfill their calling with excellence (Competencies).

All of this needs to happen for the 4/14ers in an effective, holistic transformational context. Jesus carefully created a transformational context to serve as a laboratory to prepare His emerging leaders. It was...

- A spiritual environment that was conducive towards growth in one's relationship with God (with Himself, as well as the Father through prayer).

- A relational web that involved a relationship with a mature leader/mentor (Himself) as well as relationships with other likeminded followers (the community of disciples).
- An experiential context involving challenging and diverse assignments that forced his followers to have cohesion between their "action" and their "confession."

From this transformational context Jesus instructed them and this produced nothing less than a total change of their lives and circumstances! The same careful approach will serve as an incubator for a generation of changed lives within the 4/14 window. Not only will they be more apt to live a meaningful life, they will also have found fulfillment in their relationship with God, garnered the knowledge and skills to impact tomorrow's world, and have a mission and purpose to live by.

These principles serve as a framework through which we can design programs that will transform the lives of children in the 4/14 Window. This framework can be applied in any context, and in any culture resulting in transformational impact. It is a paradigm, not a program.

Raising Up a New Generation To Transform Our World

I began this chapter with a call for a new missional focus. I said that just as the 10/40 Window focused our attention on "the core of the core," so the 4/14 Window was a focus on the core of the core. My purpose was to turn the spotlight on those in the 4/14 Window—the Ages of Opportunity. We have seen that this group is an enormous "people group"—one that is suffering, neglected and exploited. At the same time, those precious ones in the 4/14 Window are also, without question, the most receptive people group on the planet.

Both their receptivity as subjects for holistic mission, and their transformational potential as agents for transformational mission have been largely overlooked by the mission community. I said that this chapter was an urgent appeal to consider this potential, and the strategic importance of those 1.2 billion children and youth in the 4/14 Window. And it was a plea to open your heart and mind to the challenge of reaching and raising up a new generation that would be transformed and mobilized as agents to change the world.

In this document I have presented the tremendous needs and opportunities for the 4 to 14 age group to be raised up in every nation. We have seen the importance of having a holistic ministry approach to those children. And we have called the Body of Christ to give priority to reaching this age group and to mobilizing them to carry out the church's mission.

I close with another invitation to join with many others around the globe who are seeing the tremendous needs of this remarkable group. They are reading Scripture again with the "child in the midst" and are finding that not only are 4/14ers present, but indeed everywhere throughout the Bible—very often in transformational roles. They are seeing that we are to care for and nurture children because they are so close to the heart of God. They see that we must take the 4/14ers seriously, because God surely does!

Realizing the need to reprioritize my own missional focus on the 4/14 Window was a transforming moment for me, as it was for many others. "Moments of transforming significance radically reopen the question of reality."[69] I am praying that in reading this chapter you will experience your transforming moment—the instant you realize the need for change and say "yes" to intentional engagement in raising up a new generation from the 4/14 Window to change the world.

To learn more about Transform World New Generation visit: http://4to14Window.com

Endnotes

1 Christian Standard Bible (Nashville: Holman Bible Publishers, 2004).

2 Luis Bush, *The 10/40 Window: Getting to the Core of the Core*, AD2000 & Beyond, www.ad2000.org/1040broc.htm (accessed Feb. 17, 2009).

4 Bryan Nicholson, Global Mapping International (Colorado Springs, CO, 2009) using data from UNICEF.

5 Bryan Nicholson, Global Mapping International (Colorado Springs, CO, 2009) using Patrick Johnstone data prepared for two upcoming publications.

6 Ibid.

7 Jason Mandryk, "Status of the Gospel 2006," Joshua Project, http://www.joshuaproject.net/great-commissionpowerpoints.php (accessed February 17, 2009).

8 http://www.nationmaster.com/red/graph/peo_age_str_0_14_yea-age-structure-0-14-years&int=-1&b_map=1 (accessed February 20, 2009).

10 Glenn Miles and Josephine-Joy Wright, *Celebrating Children* (Kingstown Broadway, Carlisle, UK: Paternoster Press, 2003), p.130.

20 Dan Brewster, *"Themes and Implications of Holistic Child Development Programming in Seminaries,"* (paper written for Asia Theological Association (ATA) conference on Leadership in an Age of Crisis, unpublished) p.6, 51

21 Ibid.

22 James E. Katz and Mark Aakhus, ed., *Perpetual Contact: Mobile Communication, Private Talk, Public Performance*(Cambridge, UK: Cambridge University Press, 2002), p.138.

23 The World Values Survey is an ongoing academic project by social scientists to assess the state of socio-cultural, moral, religious, and political values of different cultures around the world which has produced more than 300 publications in 14 languages.

24 Susan Greener, *Celebrating Children* (Kingstown Broadway, Carlisle, UK: Paternoster Press, 2003), p.130.

25 Adapted from Bryant Myers, *"Transformational Development Course Notes,"* Fuller Theological Seminary: School of Intercultural Studies, January 2003.

26 Dan Brewster, "The 4/14 Window: Child Ministries and Mission Strategy," *Children in Crisis: A New Commitment*, ed. Phyllis Kilbourn (Monrovia, CA: MARC, 1996).

27 George Barna, *Transforming Your Children Into Spiritual Champions* (Ventura, CA: Regal Publications, 2003).

29 George Barna, "Research Shows That Spiritual Maturity Process Should Start at a Young Age," The Barna Group, http://www.barna.org/FlexPage.aspx?Page=BarnaUpdate&BarnaU pdateID=153 (accessed February 19, 2009).

30 George Barna, *Transforming Your Children Into Spiritual Champions* (Ventura, CA: Regal Publications, 2003) p.58.

31 Jean Piaget, *Stages of Intellectual Development In Children and Teenagers*, Child Development Institute, http://www.childdevelopmentinfo.com/development/piaget.shtml (accessed February 17, 2009).

32 Thomas Jefferson's definition of religion: "The duty that we owe to the Creator."

33 Samuel P. Huntington, Lawrence E. Harrison, *Culture Matters: How Values Shape Human Progress* (New York, NY: Basic Books, 2000).

34 Fareed Zakaria, "A Conversation with Lee Kuan Yew, (Palm Coast, FL: *Foreign Affairs*) March/April 1994.p.52

36 D. Gordon, et.al, Study: *Child Poverty in the Developing World* (Bristol, UK: Centre for International Poverty Research, 2003).

37 "Children on the Brink 2004 Factsheet," UNAIDS,USAID, UNICEF, http://www.unicef.org/media/files/COB_2004_fact_sheet.doc (accessed February 17,2009).

38 D. Gordon, et.al, Study: *Child Poverty in the Developing World* (Bristol, UK: Centre for International Poverty Research, 2003).

41 Ibid.

42 D. Gordon, et.al., Study: *Child Poverty in the Developing World*, (Bristol, UK: Centre for International Poverty Research, 2003).

43 Ibid.

44 Dan Brewster and Patrick McDonald, "Children: The Great Omission," Lausanne 2004 Forum, http://www.viva.org/en/articles/great_omission/great_ omission_booklet.pdf (accessed February 17,2009).

45 George Otis, Jr., "International Fellowship of Transformation Partners Definition and Values," Transform World Indonesia 2005, (May 2005).

47 Dan Brewster, "Themes and Implications of Holistic Child Development Programming in Seminaries," (paper written for Asia Theological Association (ATA)conference on Leadership in an Age of Crisis, unpublished),p.6.

49 Bryant L. Myers, *Walking with the Poor: Principles and Practices of Transformational Development* (New York: Orbis Books, 1999).

50 Chad Causley, (International Director for Global Ministries, OneHope) in discussion with the author, January2009.

51 William Damon, *Greater Expectations* (Free Press Paperbacks: New York, 1995), p.84.

52 Ibid., p.84-85

53 Ibid., p.86.

58 Alex and Brett Harris, *Do Hard Things* (Multnomah Books: Portland, 2008), p.97.

59 William Damon, *Greater Expectations* (Free Press Paperbacks: New York, 1995), p.128.

62 Robert Coles, *The Spiritual Life of Children* (Boston, MA: The Houghton Mifflin Company, 1990).

63 Roy Zuck, *Precious in His Sight* (Grand Rapids, MI: Baker Books, 1996) 201, quoting from Leon Morris, *The Gospel According to St. Luke: An Introduction and Commentary* (Grand Rapids, MI: Wm. B.

Eerdmans Publishing Co., 1974), p.226.

64 Mark 10:14

65 Dan Brewster, *Child, Church and Mission* (Colorado Springs: Compassion, 2005), p.40.

66 Jaisankar Sarma (Director of World Vision Transformation Development International; International Director for Transformation Development; Facilitator Transformation Indicators Task Force for WVI), Personal interview in Washington DC, 25 January 2006.

67 Ibid.

68 Malcolm Webber, "The ConneXions Model," adapted with permission of Malcolm Webber, Leader Source SGA. For the complete models see Healthy Leaders: Spirit-Built Leadership #2, and Building Leaders: Spirit-Built Leadership #4, www.leadersource.org andwww.leadershipletters.com.

69 James E. Loder, *The Transforming Moment* (Colorado Springs, CO: Helmers & Howard Publishers, 1989), back cover.

PRAYER STATIONS GUIDE
ON THE MILLENNIUM DEVELOPMENT GOALS (MDGs)

Micah Challenge[1]

Introduction

In 2000, the nations of the world, including the United States, adopted eight Millennium Development Goals (MDGs) for the alleviation of extreme poverty. Targets were set for each of these goals, and nations have made commitments for meeting these targets by 2015. The MDG Prayer Stations in this booklet are interactive prayer activities designed for small and large groups of people. The stations invite participants to take time to reflect and engage with the issues of global poverty, bringing them to God in prayer.

Micah Challenge is grounded in the spirit of Micah 6:8, "And what does the Lord require of you? To act justly and to love mercy and to walk humbly with your God."

This Guide will help you set up the Millennium Development Goals prayer station activities for group use. Participants can be invited to reflect on the stations at their own pace, with the freedom to interact with as many of the activities as they wish. You can place copies of the story, activity, prayer and scripture at each station, or you may choose to provide a copy of the Guide for each participant. This guide can also be used independently as a guide to personal prayer.

---

[1] The MDG Prayer Guide is an offering of Micah Challenge USA, adapted with permission from a resource created by Micah Challenge Australia.

We hope this guide inspires your activism and nurtures your contemplative spirit.
Micah Challenge is a global campaign to mobilize Christians against poverty. The campaign aims to deepen Christian engagement with impoverished and marginalized communities, and to influence leaders of rich and poor nations to fulfill their promise to achieve the Millennium Development Goals. Micah Challenge exists in 39 countries around the globe.

"This is a moment in history when the stated intentions of world leaders echo the Biblical prophets and the teachings of Jesus—a time when we have the means to dramatically reduce poverty..." *—Excerpt from The Micah Call*

Prayer
Why Prayer?
Prayer needs to be an important part of our efforts to overcome extreme poverty. We pray for the MDGs because prayer:

- Brings our hearts closer to the heart of God, especially as it concerns the poor. God's grace inspires us to strive for justice when we pray.

- Helps us remember that real people are behind every staggering poverty statistic.

- Sustains us as we seek to overcome the injustice of global poverty.

- Empowers us to be POWERFUL agents of social change.

How to Get More Involved
- Set up a Micah Challenge resource station inviting people to sign the Micah Call (www.micahchallenge.us) and sign up to receive weekly Micah Challenge Friday

Prayer reflection emails.

- Plan a time for writing letters to elected officials on relevant MDG legislation.

- Follow the prayer station experience with small group discussion and prayer based on the participants' experience.

- Invite the group to develop an action plan forgetting involved in the Micah Challenge to overcome extreme global poverty.

- For other ideas on how to use this resource to engage your community, visit: www.micahchallenge.us or e-mailinfo@micahchallenge.us.

- Let us know when you use this resource or host this activity with your church, campus or network. Your feedback is important!

Goal 1: Eradicate Extreme Poverty and Hunger

Nearly one billion people live on less than $1 a day. In the Democratic Republic of Congo, a boy spends every day chipping through stones in search of minerals to sell. For a flour bag of mineral-rich stones he is paid as little as 25 cents. His family and community are dependent on this industry.

Activity 1

Break a piece off the rubble with the hammer as a prayer to bring daily bread to this community.
Preparation: hammer, bricks, rubble or rocks.

Target for Goal 1

Halve, between 1990 and 2015, the proportion of people whose income is less than $1 a day and those who suffer from hunger.

Pray

- For justice for Africa, the world's poorest continent, where one in three people are malnourished. About half of its nearly 700 million people live on less than $1 a day; most (80 percent) live on less than $2 a day.

- For the leaders of the world's richest countries, that the aid they have promised impoverished nations will be delivered and that the crippling debts still owed by these same countries will be cancelled.

Bible Witness

Suppose a brother or a sister is without clothes and daily food. If one of you says to him, "Go, I wish you well; keep warm and well fed," but does nothing about his physical needs, what good is it? In the same way, faith by itself, if it is not accompanied by action, is dead. – James 2:15-17[2]

Goal 2: Achieve Universal Primary Education

Rowena was three when she started work in the Philippines, digging through a garbage dump to collect recyclable materials. She's never been to school at all.

Activity 2

Think about how education has empowered you. On one page, write or draw something you have learned in the past year. On another page, write or draw a prayer for children like Rowena who have not had the opportunity to finish, or even begin, primary school.

Preparation: a notebook (or two if there are a lot of people), pens or pencils.

---

[2] All Scripture quotations are taken from the *Holy Bible: New International Version.* ·Copyright 1973, 1978, 1984 International Bible Society. Used by permission of Zondervan. All rights reserved.

Target for Goal 2

Ensure that, by 2015, children everywhere, boys and girls alike, will be able to complete a full course of primary schooling.

Pray

- That parents in impoverished countries will not be forced to choose between sending their children to school or sending them to work to enable the family to survive.
- That, across the globe, girls' education will be valued equally with boys' education.

Bible Witness

And Jesus grew in wisdom and stature, and in favor with God and men. —Luke 2:52

Goal 3: Promote Gender Equality and Empower Women

At fourteen, Phally was working two jobs while her brothers went to school. Now, with the help of a small loan and some training, she runs a successful grocery business in Cambodia, employs her brothers, and can send her own daughter to school.

Activity 3

As a prayer for the empowerment of women around the world, help a woman (red) stand equal with a man (blue).

Preparation: sticks (go scavenging in your neighborhood!), a large tray of sand or dirt to bury the sticks in. Wet the sand a little so the sticks stand up better. Tie red ribbon around half the sticks, blue around the other half. Stand the blue sticks up right in the sand and bury the red sticks.

Target for Goal 3

Eliminate gender disparity in primary and secondary education, preferably by 2005, and in all levels of education no later than 2015.

Pray

- That girls will be able to choose the time of their own marriage and that it will not necessitate sacrificing their schooling.

- For more female teachers to be trained in countries where there are cultural constraints against women's education.

Bible Witness

There is neither Jew nor Greek, slave nor free, male nor female, for you are all one in Christ Jesus.—Galatians 3:28

Goal 4: Reduce Child Mortality

In Afghanistan each year, 283,000 children under the age of five die. Bismillah is one of the fortunate ones. Suffering malnourishment and pneumonia, she was brought in time to a clinic where she's on her way to recovery.

Activity 4

Take a clay baby and mould it into a grown person as a prayer to reduce the mortality rate among children under five.
Preparation: modeling clay or play-doh. Have clay molded into babies, ready for people to use.

Target for Goal 4

Reduce by two-thirds, between 1990 and 2015, the under-five mortality rate.

Pray

- For the provision of simple rehydration solutions to treat diarrhea, which accounts for one in six of the 10.6 million child deaths worldwide each year.
- For the success of World Food Program's activities to prevent under-nutrition, which is an underlying cause in

more than half of all the above deaths before age 5.

- For the provision of mosquito nets in Africa, where 94 percent of all child deaths attributed to malaria occur.

Bible Witness
He took a little child and had him stand among them. Taking him in his arms, he said to them, "Whoever welcomes these little children in my name welcomes me; and whoever welcomes me does not welcome me but the one who sent me."—Mark 9:36-37

Goal 5: Improve Maternal Health
Around 529,000 women die each year giving birth; 99 percent are from developing countries and 80 percent of the deaths are preventable. As a traditional birth attendant, Emily is fighting to reverse these statistics, helping with safer deliveries for hundreds of women in rural Malawi.

Activity 5
Take two pieces of small stationery. On the first sheet, write a short note of gratitude to the maternal figure in your life. On the second sheet, write a short prayer for someone who had to grow up without a mother because she died during childbirth.

Preparation: Two stacks of stationery or notepaper, pens or pencils.

Pray
- For the training of more traditional birthing attendants where there is a shortage of trained midwives.
- For the decrease of Female Genital Mutilation, which can contribute to prolonged or obstructed labor.
- Especially for women in sub-Saharan Africa, who face a one-in-13 chance of dying during pregnancy and childbirth, while for women in the industrialized world the risk is only one-in-4,085.

Bible Witness

"The Holy Spirit will come upon you, and the power of the Most High will overshadow you. So the holy one to be born will be called the Son of God. Even Elizabeth your relative is going to have a child in her old age, and she who was said to be barren is in her sixth month. For nothing is impossible with God."—Luke 1:35-37

Goal 6: Combat HIV/AIDS, Malaria and Other Diseases

Pedro, Rose and Chembe visit the grave of their mother who died from an HIV/AIDS illness. Their grandfather now takes care of them. Over 14 million children have been orphaned by HIV/AIDS worldwide.

Activity 6

Remove a marble from the red liquid and place it on the blue cloth as a prayer to halt and begin to reverse the spread of HIV/AIDS.
Preparation: one large bowl, water, red food coloring, marbles, a piece of colored cloth.

Target for Goal 6

Have halted and begun to reverse the spread of HIV/AIDS and begun to reverse the incidence of malaria and other major diseases by 2015.

Pray

- For the empowerment of women in the global south, who often have no choice over the timing or manner of sex.
- For Western governments and pharmaceutical companies to show compassion in allowing inexpensive anti-retroviral drugs to be made available in impoverished countries.
- For the rescue of trafficked women and children, who are often forced into sexual slavery and thus exposed to the HIV virus.

Bible Witness

Jesus went throughout Galilee, teaching in their synagogues, preaching the good news of the kingdom, and healing every disease and sickness among the people. – Matthew 4:23

"I needed clothes and you clothed me, I was sick and you looked after me, I was in prison and you came to visit me." – Matthew 25:36

Goal 7: Ensure Environmental Sustainability

Every day Mame collects water for her family in Senegal. She's lucky enough to live near a bore hole. The average distance to travel for water in Africa is 6 km, and some children spend up to six hours per day on this task.

Activity 7

Take away a stone from their road to make the distance shorter, and use it to begin building a well for the 1.2 billion people worldwide who have no access to clean water.

Preparation: string to outline the base of the well, along with stones, rocks or sugar cubes.

Targets for Goal 7

Integrate the principles of sustainable development into country policies and programs, and reverse the loss of environmental resources. Halve, by 2015, the proportion of people without sustainable access to safe drinking water and basic sanitation.

Pray

- For development agencies, that they achieve further success in implementing sustainable agriculture and industry policies.
- That countries of the global south will not be forced into privatizing water supplies which would then be provided for profit rather than as a public service.

Bible Witness

The poor and needy search for water, but there is none; their tongues are parched with thirst. But I the Lord will answer them; I, the God of Israel, will not forsake them. I will make rivers flow on barren heights, and springs within the valleys. I will turn the desert into pools of waters, and the parched ground into springs.—Isaiah 41:17-18

Goal 8: Develop a Global Partnership for Development

In Uganda, Simon sells the harvest from a few parched coffee plants that his parents planted before their death. He has no access to global markets or opportunity for a fair price. For every $1 paid for coffee or tea at a supermarket, less than 15 cents goes to people in the country where the tea was grown.

Activity 8

Drink a cup of Fair Trade coffee or tea and give producers, blenders and packers in poorer countries a fair deal. As you drink, pray for rich countries to recognize their responsibility to work for justice for the poor.

Preparation: Fair Trade coffee or tea bags, cups, coffee maker, hot water, sugar, milk.

Targets for Goal 8

Deal comprehensively with the debt problems of developing countries through national and international measures in order to make debt sustainable in the long term. Address the least developed countries' special needs. This includes tariff- and quota-free access for their exports; enhanced debt relief for heavily indebted poor countries; cancellation of official bilateral debt; and more generous official development assistance for countries committed to poverty reduction.

Pray

- For those involved in reforming international trade systems, that poorer producers will have fair trading access and get a reasonable price for their goods from richer countries.
- For those all around the world who are working with the poor, that they may know God's power as they bring change and hope in culturally appropriate ways.

Bible Witness

"Why have we fasted," they say, "and you have not seen it? Why have we humbled ourselves, and you have not noticed? Your fasting ends in quarreling and strife, and in striking each other with wicked fists. You cannot fast as you do today and expect your voice to be heard on high."—Isaiah 58:3-4

A poor man's field may produce abundant food, but injustice sweeps it away.—Proverbs 13:23

To become involved with Micah Challenge USA, visit www.micahchallenge.us

Micah Challenge USA Steering Committee:

- Baptist World Alliance
- Bread for the World
- Christian Reformed Church of North America
- Cooperative Baptist Fellowship
- Emergent Village
- Episcopalians for Global Reconciliation
- Evangelicals for Social Action
- Millennium Campaign
- National Association of Evangelicals
- Salvation Army World Services Division

- Sojourners
- World Hope International
- World Relief
- World Vision

Micah Challenge Partners With:

- Covenant World Relief/Evangelical Covenant Church
- Food for the Hungry
- Jubilee USA
- The ONE Campaign
- World Concern

Reprinted with permission from Micah Challenge: Prayer Stations Guide on the Millennium Development Goals. ©2009 by Micah Challenge US and Micah Challenge Australia.

Discovering and Addressing the Root Causes of Genocide in Rwanda

James Butare-Kiyovu

The Need for a Different Look at "History"
A Kinyarwanda Legend:

Long before the colonial era and the introduction of Christianity, Rwandans believed in one God the Creator, *(Imana Rurema)*.

A Kinyarwanda legend says that God created three brothers: Gatwa, Gahutu and Gatutsi. The prefix Ga- denotes a brotherly endearment. The three brothers shared and still share everything in common: the same language, the same culture, the same traditions etc.

One day, God told the three brothers that he was going on a long journey. He left a jug full of milk to each of the three brothers and told them to keep their milk until his return.

After some time, Gatwa the youngest of the brothers started playing and ended up spilling his milk. Gahutu felt hungry and thirsty and decided to drink his milk. Gatutsi kept the milk.

When God returned he told the three brothers that because Gatutsi had obeyed him and kept the milk, he would be in charge of his younger brothers. God gave him cows that had produced the milk, and that became the symbol of his stewardship and protection over his two brothers.

That legend (abridged for purposes of this paper) kept the three brothers living harmoniously together for centuries before the coming of the Germans, the first colonial masters to rule Rwanda. The legend can also be used to gain useful insights in the following complex systems that existed in pre-colonial Rwanda.

Kinship System: All Rwandans whether Hutu or Tutsi belong to various kinship groupings and lineages, such as *abega, abasindi, abasinga,* except for the Banyiginya, which was exclusive to the royal family.

Feudal System: In Rwanda there was a hereditary system of kings (*abami*), chiefs and sub-chiefs (*abatware*) who exercised the political and military administration of the country.

Ubuhake: This was a Master-Servant relationship that characterized the social system in pre-colonial Rwanda. It was based on the ownership of cattle and land. If you were a rich landowner with many cows, you would afford to have many servants (*abagaragu*). Under the "ubuhake" feudal system the master did not "own" the servant, in the same way a master owned a slave in countries that practiced slave trade and slavery. The relationship could be terminated, especially if the master failed to give the expected cow/cows and protection to the servant for the work accomplished. Apart from very few top aristocratic families, every Rwandan whether Tutsi, Hutu or Twa was answerable to someone else above him in this system of ubuhake.

Creation of the "Hima-Tutsi Empire" myth: When colonialists arrived in Rwanda, they were surprised to find a well-organized hierarchical leadership under a King (*Umwami*), which resembled in many ways the feudal Kingdoms in European countries. They started speculating that the Tutsis, especially the King and his chiefs (*abatware*) with whom they were in contact, could not be of the same origin as the people they ruled. They wrote their speculations in books, claiming among other things that Hutus were Bantu while Tutsis were

Hamitic. They speculated that the Tutsis had come from somewhere north, probably from Ethiopia or Egypt herding their cattle along the river Nile. Their theory appeared to them all the more plausible because they found similar kingdoms in the Great Lakes Region, notably the Hima/Huma in Uganda and Burundi who seemed to have the same morphological features and also seemed to share the same customs and traditions.

The Indirect Rule Policy: The Germans who ruled Rwanda before they lost the First World War and the Belgians who replaced them decided to practice the so called *Indirect Rule Policy* whereby the traditional feudal system under the King and his chiefs was allowed to run side by side with the colonial system. The Tutsis, especially those in the higher ranks of the feudal system, had more access to the colonial education and to the colonial jobs. That colonial advantage considerably widened the gap, which already existed because of the inherent inequality in any feudal system.

Revival vs. Inch-deep Christianity: A vast number of people in Rwanda (about 50% of the population) became and still consider themselves Roman Catholic. During the colonial times and until very recently most Roman Catholics were not known to read the Bible for themselves. Unfortunately the words the catholic priests recited (mostly on Sundays in Latin) could not be fully understood by the large majority of the attendants. As a result, there is a great need for Christian growth in Rwanda beyond the inch-deep understanding of the Scriptures. At the same time, there was growth and revival amongst some Rwandan Protestant denominations (about 30% of the population) who read the Bible and/or listen to someone reading the Bible in their own mother tongue, Kinyarwanda.

Bad Leadership: The educated Tutsis who had cohabited with the Belgian masters during the colonial era were the same ones who started agitating for independence. This happened in the late 1950's, when Congo and Burundi were also looking for independence. In 1956 the ruling Tutsi council sent a document to the UN asking for political autonomy. Belgium, which is roughly the same size as Rwanda, was not ready to hand over power and riches from her colonies, without a fight. As far as Rwanda is concerned, there was an about-turn in the Belgian politics. In retaliation, the Belgian administration decided to support a few educated Hutus and helped them to revolt against the monarchy. In 1957, that group of educated Hutus around Gregoire Kayibanda published "The Hutu Manifesto" which called for the abolition of Tutsi privileges.

In 1959 after the death of King Mutara, a succession of events in Rwanda led to thousands of Tutsis being killed by Hutus while others became refugees especially in the neighboring countries of Uganda, Burundi, Congo and Tanzania. Tutsis who stayed in Rwanda became second-class citizens in their country and constantly faced physical and psychological harassments.

Distorted History: After the first attempt of genocide against the Tutsis and their exile in the 1960's the leadership in Rwanda started teaching a distorted history in order to justify their discrimination against the Tutsis. "The Hima-Tutsi Empire" speculations first made by colonialists were now taught in schools as historical facts. In my opinion, such speculations were most unfortunate but I don't believe in any way that they constituted a conscious "systematic planning of genocide" at the time.

Every time the regime faced some obstacle, the Tutsis were used as a scarecrow to eliminate them. The Tutsis were vilified and referred to as *inzoka* snakes and/or *inyenzi* cockroaches. Since killing a snake or a cockroach is normal and expected, those who killed Tutsis got away with it. Many Hutus after independence developed a mentality of impunity as far as killing or mistreating a Tutsi was concerned. The euphemism for killing a Tutsi was referred to as *gukora* meaning "doing useful work."

The Cold-War Factor: It would be difficult to justify that Westerners (including missionaries) that lived and had embassies and projects in Rwanda did not know what was happening. One reason, which may explain their silence or in some cases their open support to the Hutu extremist regimes, is the cold war factor. The first President of Rwanda, Gregoire Kayibanda was a former Roman Catholic seminarian who kept strong ties with the Catholic Church and with the Belgian Government.

The second President of Rwanda, Juvenal Habyarimana, was also considered a very devout Catholic and a friend of the West. Both had full protection from the West because they claimed to stand against communism. Western countries therefore ignored or turned a blind eye to the gross injustices and killings that were happening in Rwanda. That was also true with other countries such as Zaire (now the Democratic Republic of Congo) that were not aligned to the Soviet Union and communism. When the cold war period ended and the West started withdrawing the unconditional support, most of those regimes collapsed one after the other.

The Refugee Factor: For over thirty years, Rwandans (mainly Tutsis) lived in exile, the vast majority of them in refugee camps. Both the first Republic of President Kayibanda and the second Republic of Habyarimana refused to do anything about settling the refugee issue. Their argument was that Rwanda is a small country and therefore refugees had to remain where they were. In the 1960's when the refugees made desperate and poorly organized attacks into Rwanda, the Tutsis inside the country were killed or persecuted. In the late 1970 when a younger generation of Rwandans formed a political organization that later became the Rwandans Patriotic Front (RPF) the regime in Rwanda still refused to have anything to do with them, totally convinced that they could not be a threat.

Genocide

Picture in your mind two women. One woman with a raised machete chasing another woman carrying a baby on her back. Let your mind focus for a moment on the two women and then briefly shift to a group of UN soldiers who are intently watching the chase. The UN soldiers are heavily armed. They have armored personnel carriers (APCs), which are labelled UN in big white letters. Then go back to the two women. The one with the machete has considerably gained ground on the one fleeing with her baby. Then, a ghastly thing happens. The woman with the baby has fallen down and the other woman is repeatedly cutting up the mother and the baby with the machete. Go back to the UN soldiers. They look horrified but none has moved.

During the Rwandan genocide, which took place from April to July 1994, I was still the RPF (Rwandese Patriotic Front) representative and my office was strategically placed in Brussels, Belgium. I had been part of the RPF and Government of Rwanda Joint Mission to UN in New York that had led to the UN Security Council Resolution 872. According to the resolution, the UN peacekeepers in Rwanda were not supposed to take sides. But ... how if the UN soldiers had decided to shoot in the air? Probably the woman with a baby could have escaped. Probably the genocide would not have taken place.

There was also the shocking news of the killing of ten Belgian peacekeepers, along with Ms. Agathe Uwilingiyimana, the Prime Minister, they were charged to protect. I remember being summoned to the Belgian Ministry of Foreign Affairs. The message to the RPF organization was short and final. The remaining Belgian peacekeepers were pulling out of Rwanda.

Within days, the French Government and other Western governments started evacuating their nationals. We in RPF felt angry and scandalized that the UN Security Council could continue to sit in the company of the Rwandan ambassador and for weeks resist to use the term "genocide" when the massacres were claiming thousands and thousands of mainly Tutsi people everyday. If that was not genocide, then what was it?

In an article commemorating ten years after the genocide, Sir Edward Clay, then High Commissioner to Uganda and non-resident Ambassador to Rwanda recalls: "It was not until the massacres of 1994 were well advanced that I and others even began to speak of genocide. Some had warned us in advance that this was planned. Failing to recognize the validity of those warnings was at least a failure of information and of understanding and analysis."

The UN Security Council persisted with their flawed analysis of the situation and decided to reduce the UNAMIR (United Nations Assistance Mission in Rwanda) comprising at the time of 2,500 soldiers under the command of Canadian Major General Romeo Dallaire to only 450 personnel. The violence that followed was unprecedented in the history of Rwanda and in the history of the world. One million people, mainly Tutsis, were brutally killed in a matter of a hundred days.

The Rwandan genocide did not result from a spontaneous outburst of anger because of President Habyarimana's death, as some people think. It was a very well prepared and very well executed genocide. And ... the powers that be did not fail to stop it for lack of information. The RPF office in Brussels, among others, sent out numerous press releases to the media, embassies in Brussels, ministries, international organizations, NGO's, political parties, church leaders, etc., warning of the systematic preparations of the genocide and the training and arming of the Interahamwe militia.

My office also distributed evidence of systematic propaganda by Hutu extremists who were using the hate radio RTLM and hate magazines. It was particularly shocking to read the "Hutu ten commandments" in one of the more virulent extremist publications called "Kangura." It was clear that a few evil people were playing on the ignorance of the Rwandan mostly illiterate population. Their strategy was to make them think that there was some Biblical justification for their extermination plans ... and they succeeded.

What Lessons Can Missions Learn from the Rwandan Genocide?

All religious missions in Rwanda at the time of genocide responded to the call of their governments for immediate evacuation, just like the rest of their fellow international community. Tutsi co-workers in churches, hospitals and other mission projects were shocked to be abandoned when it was clear they faced certain death. But ...is it reasonable to expect any help from missions in such a situation? What can missions do when UN and Governments fail?

Hugh McCullum (1994:75) recorded in his book subtitled *The Rwanda Tragedy and the Churches* a testimony from a Rwandan pastor which shows the weaknesses of the Rwandan Church [and if I may suggest the weaknesses of the missions too] during the post independence rule to the time of genocide. (1962 to 1994).

The pastor lamented:

> Why did the message of the gospel not reach the people who were baptized? What did we lose? We lost our lives. We lost our credibility. We are ashamed. We are weak. But, most of all, we lost our prophetic mission. *We could not go to the President and tell him the truth because we became sycophants to the authorities.*

> We have had killings here since 1959. *No one condemned them.* During the First Republic, they killed slowly, slowly, but *no one from the churches spoke out. No one spoke on behalf of those killed.* During the Second Republic there were more killings and more people were tortured and raped and disappeared; and *we did not speak out because we were afraid, and because we were comfortable.*

Now there has to be a new start, a new way. We must accept that Jesus' mission to us to preach the gospel means that we must be ready to protect the sheep, the flock—even if it means we must risk our lives - to lay down our lives for our sisters and brothers. *The Bible does not know Hutu and Tutsi, neither should we.* [*My emphasis in italics*]

The international community has recognized its failure. For example, during a visit to Africa in 1998, President Clinton apologized to the people of Rwanda. He said: "All over the world there were people like me sitting in offices who did not fully appreciate the depth and the speed with which you were being engulfed by this unimaginable terror."

The United Nations has also recognized its failure and has designated April 7 (day when the massacres started) as the International Day of Reflection on the Genocide in Rwanda. The UN has also established an International Criminal Tribunal on Rwanda (based in Arusha, Tanzania), and all countries are expected to search for and prosecute those accused of genocide.

What Attitude Should Missions Take?

On 19th February 2003 Elizaphan Ntakirutimana, a senior Pastor with the Seventh-Day Adventist Church in Mugonero, was convicted of aiding and abetting in genocide. His son Gerard Ntakirutimana, a medical doctor, was convicted of genocide and crimes against humanity. Both had found refuge and were living peacefully in USA before being extradited to Arusha.

Two Benedictine nuns, Consolate Mukangango and Julienne Mukabutera, who used to run the convent in Sovu, collaborated with the killers by providing them with the petrol that set the building on fire where 500 Tutsi were hiding. A Brussels court has sentenced them to 15 and 12 years respectively.

Other religious people have been arrested and are still awaiting trial. Many others are known to be still at large. It is a very sad situation to see former colleagues being pursued for genocide related crimes. However, it is also a sobering reminder that denominational Churches and missions in the West should make sure that they are not playing host to innocent-looking associates who may have taken part in crimes against humanity.

Are Poverty and Ignorance the Root Problems?

Some people argue that Africa's poverty increases the competition for what resources there are within the country and this may have been one of the factors that caused the Rwandan genocide. It is true that most of the militia were unemployed youths who were promised money, jobs or land and property that belonged to the Tutsis. There was also evidence that most of them killed under the influence of alcohol and other drug substances provided by the organizers.

Others argue that ignorance was at the root of the problems in Rwanda. For example, it was ignorance that caused hatred that led millions of illiterate and semi-illiterate Rwandans to believe in the distortions that were made by highly intelligent but evil extremists concerning the Hutu Ten Commandments.

Change of Attitude Is Necessary in Order to Address the Root Problem

In the November-December 2007 Mission Frontiers, Chris Page quoted from Darrow Miller's book *Discipling Nations* where it says that except for catastrophic events such as war, drought, floods, earthquakes etc., *physical poverty doesn't "just happen."* He says it's the logical result of the way people look at themselves and the world, the stories that they tell to make sense of their world. Physical poverty is rooted in a mindset of poverty, a set of ideas held corporately that produce certain behaviors. These behaviors can be institutionalized into the laws and structures of society. The consequence of these behaviors and structures is poverty.

Chris Page goes on to compare Rwanda's President Paul Kagame, whom he says has demonstrated the example of a hard-working man, standing against corruption, and planning ahead with a visionary attitude of what could be if we work at it with all our effort.

Page correctly observed that previous leaders of Rwanda either had the attitude regarding their country of "We are poor. We will always be poor, and there is nothing we can do about it" (which is fatalism), or, "We are poor because others made us poor. They are going to have to solve our problem. We cannot solve our problems."

Page offers another insightful observation that the majority of Rwandans at the moment still have this attitude, especially about themselves. Some people in the West still have this attitude, but it's the minority, not the majority.

I believe that UN and good political leadership, alone, will not address the problem of poor attitudes. The Church has an even more important role to play in order to restore people's "damaged identities."

I also believe that Churches and Non-Government Organisations, committed to preach and to practice "integral mission or holistic transformation" and "Shalom" discussed in this book, will be more suited to address the root problems of the so called "Bottom Billion" people.

Definition

LEGEND:
1. A non-historical or unverifiable story handed down by tradition from earlier times and popularly accepted as historical.
2. The body of stories of this kind, especially as they relate to a particular people or group or clan.

References

Butare-Kiyovu, James
    2004 Ethnic Factor in the World Today: Rwanda's Genocide. In Insight Course. William Carey International University.

2002 A collection of modules on: Scripture Use; Literacy; Community Development and Peacemaking. The curriculum has been translated from English into Kinyarwanda.

"Hutu Ten Commandments" created by Hassan Ngeze, the producer of hate newspaper Kagura, First published in December 1990 (Kangura, N. 6). Available from www.google.com; INTERNET.

Internews. 2002. "Nahimana Led Anti – Tutsi Committee, Expert Witness Says" Available from www.allAfrica.com INTERNET.

McCullum, Hugh

1994 *The Angels Have Left Us. The Rwandese Tragedy and the Churches.* Geneva: WCC Publications.

New Vision. 2002. "No Plot for Hima, Tutsi Empire – Museveni." Available from www.allAfrica.com INTERNET.

The East African. 2002. "Why US Didn't Stop Kigali Genocide." Available from www.allAfrica.com INTERNET.

The East African. 2004. "What Clinton Knew About Rwanda Genocide." Available from www.allAfrica.com INTERNET.

The Nation (Nairobi). 2005. "Time to Remember Rwanda Genocide." Available from www.allAfrica.com INTERNET.

The New Times (Kigali). 2006. "What Next? Do You Profit from Distorting Rwanda Issues." Available from www.allAfrica.com INTERNET.

* 9 7 8 0 8 6 5 8 5 0 2 8 6 *